Healing In The Presence of The Lord

Natalie Degraffinreaidt

Healing in the Presence of the Lord

Copyright © 2016 by Natalie Degraffinreaidt

All rights reserved. No part of this book may be reproduced or transmitted in any form or by any means without written permission of the author.

King James Version, Scripture quotations marked "KJV" are taken from the Holy Bible, King James Version (Public Domain).

Scripture quotations marked "ESV" are from the ESV Bible® (The Holy Bible: English Standard Version®), copyright © 2001 by Crossway Bibles, a publishing ministry of Good News Publishers. Used by permission. All rights reserved. http://www.crossway.org

Scripture quotations marked "NIV" are taken from the Holy Bible, New International Version®, NIV®. Copyright © 1973, 1978, 1984 by Biblica, Inc. TM Used by permission of Zondervan. All rights reserved worldwide. http://www.zondervan.com

Scripture quotations marked "NLT" are taken from the Holy Bible, New Living Translation, copyright © 1996, 2004, 2007 by Tyndale House Foundation. Used by permission of Tyndale House Publishers, Inc., Carol Stream, Illinois 60188. All rights reserved.
http://www.newlivingtranslation.com/ http://www.tyndale.com

ISBN 9780996404068

Library of Congress Control Number: 2016938245

Book published by:

Kingdom Kaught Publishing LLC
Denton, MD 21629
First printed in the U.S.A.

Dedication

I would like to dedicate this book to every person who is struggling with self-esteem issues, self-identity problems, teenage pregnancy, verbal, sexual, mental, drug, or physical abuse. This dedication goes out to newlyweds and older married couples, too!

I pray this book will enable someone to be delivered from their current situation. I have poured my heart out in this book (being transparent), so another person can receive their healing! As you read this book meditate on your own issues, and see what areas you need to be set free from in your life.

The only reason this book was written is to save other souls who suffer from the things I've suffered from in my life on my journey to self-discovery in Jesus Christ. In spite of what many may think or say, it is not my intent to use this book to bash anyone. I want the truth to be told, so others can gain their freedom!

Acknowledgments

There are so many people I need to thank! If it wasn't for all of you this book wouldn't have been completed! First, I would like to thank the Lord for changing my life by healing me from my past.

I would like to thank every Pastor who poured into my life along the way, specifically, Pastor Lewis and First Lady Shirley Lewis (Christ is the Answer Deliverance Center) and, Pastor Sharps and First Lady Latandria (Jesus Lives Ministry). A special thanks to Bishop Antonio Palmer and First Lady Barbara Palmer (Kingdom Celebration Center). All of you have been blessings in my life. God placed all of you in my life during different seasons! I am forever grateful for all of you. I pray God continues to bless all of you in such a mighty way!

I thank God for my wonderful husband (Warren Degraffinreaidt, Jr). What would I do without you? We have been through the struggle together, and there have been times that we both wanted to give up but held on! We have grown together and are still growing together learning each other even more now than ever! You accepted me in spite of my mess, and I accepted you, too!

You are all mine and I belong to you. We are far from perfect, but are perfect for one another. Warren Degraffinreaidt you complete me! I can't imagine life without you by my side! You are my life. People don't understand the struggle we endured together and are still enduring, but it molded us into the people we are today!

You have played such a major role in my life. I can't thank God enough for loving me enough to send you to help heal my heart. I want you to know no matter what our past was it doesn't measure up to what our future is going to be! You have such a big heart and the love you have for people is like no other. I know the true you, people look at your outer appearance and judge you, but I know you, baby! You are my king! I want you to know all the years to come are going to be full of my love! My love will be poured out upon you like a sweet scent!

I will be that virtuous wife by your side! You will have my support in all of your life's endeavors! My love for you is pure and uncontaminated. My heart is full of the goodness of the Lord for your life, baby! I love you and just know the best is yet to come! We are breaking all generational curses as we walk into a new life for our family! You are the one!

I thank all of my children: Terrell Hopkins, Warren Degraffinreaidt lll, Airannah Degraffinreaidt, and Quincy Degraffinreaidt for being patient with their mother. I know plenty of mistakes were made along the way, but I want you to know the best is yet to come. I'm working hard to leave a legacy behind for each one of you! I am fighting hard for your futures! You guys will be successful and won't fall victim to this thing called life. I love each one of you so much. I thank the Lord for entrusting me with such wonderful gifts! You guys are the best…I'm so proud of all of you!

I want to thank my parents for being there for my family and supporting us along the way! You guys always gave your children whatever you had even if it was your last. I thank you for working hard to keep us safe to your best ability! John and Lottie Hopkins both of you are so appreciated more than words can express! You guys deserve the best. In spite of the struggle and the things that were lacking in your lives…you worked hard to make sure your children didn't lack for anything. You did the best you could with what you had. Just know all of your hard work has not gone unnoticed in our lives. I don't know what my family would do without you. I would like to thank my husband's parents, as well, for all of their help along the way in supporting us: Warren Degraffinreaidt, Sr. and Janice Degraffinreaidt! I also thank all of our family: sisters and brothers…you guys are the best!

    I can't forget everyone that helped us along the way. There are too many names to mention. Just know that all of you are truly appreciated more than you will ever know! We love each one of you who contributed to my family's life. A shout out goes to my girls: Zenda Galloway and Jamice Holley!! I love you ladies; we have been through so much together and learned from one another! I wouldn't trade you ladies for the world!!

Table of Contents

Introduction 11

Chapter 1 - **Childhood Crisis** 15

Chapter 2 - **Teenage Pregnancy** 27

Chapter 3 - **Self-Identity Crisis** 35

Chapter 4 - **The Idle Mind is the Devil's Playground** 41

Chapter 5 - **Fear** 51

Chapter 6 - **Drugs** 55

Chapter 7 - **Marriage** 59

Chapter 8 - **Being a Wife** 63

Chapter 9 - **The Rotten Wife** 67

Chapter 10 - **The Battered Wife** 73

Chapter 11 - **Walking into My Healing** 77

Chapter 12 - **Forgiving** 81

Chapter 13 - **Deliverance** 85

Chapter 14 - **Connections** 93

Chapter 15 - **Obedience** 99

Chapter 16 - **In Closing** 101

Scripture References 105

About the Author 113

Introduction

Healing in the Presence of the Lord

We are going to go through the pain of being physically, emotionally, and spiritually, lost while we're on our journey to find out who we are in Christ.

People are always going to have something to say, so we should understand that we can never please everybody. There is a verse in a song, based loosely on Matthew 7:23-27, that states "On Christ the solid Rock I stand, all other ground is sinking sand. All other ground is sinking sand." So don't build your house based on the foundation of men's opinions because without Christ you will be disappointed.

God has called us to be set apart on a holy mission to walk in His image through His Son Jesus who paid the ultimate price for our sins. God is the Creator and He has called us to spread His Truth amongst the other lost souls who haven't been healed by Him. Therefore we must always be careful of who we are connected with and who we allow to pour into our lives. Not everyone who says they are with us is. Some are small-minded people who want to keep us in a box to continue sucking the life out of us!

I wasn't always saved, but I thank God for looking down on the lowest part of the earth to pull me up from the pits of hell. Since I have been healed by God there is no way that I, as a child of God, can't show that same love and compassion to others that God has shown to me.

It's by Grace that we have been saved… not by works. Never forget where you came from because everything you've been through is not just for yourself. It's for the Divine purpose of God; not because you chose Him, but *He* chose you before the beginning of time. To know that God has chosen us to be a part of His plan for creation is something to be excited about!

There is no other love like the Love of Jesus. People looked at my circumstances from the outer appearance and dismissed me. God looked at my deeply wounded heart, and knew that all I wanted to do was to live right by Him. In order for me to live according to His purpose I needed to be healed and immersed in His Love.

I had to come to Him knocking at the door uncovered, exposing everything that wasn't right, so He could give me a permanent healing. I had been covering my wounds with make-up and clothing, but God knew I needed His Grace and Mercy.

I was tired, weak, and my strength almost gone when I started to seek Him whole-heartedly, asking for His help. He was there the whole time, and He washed me in the Living Waters of His Spirit. The water that overflows in the depths of our born-again souls bringing everlasting joy, peace, love, patience, self-discipline, gratefulness, and forgiveness.

According to Romans 8:28 (NIV), "And we know in all things God works for the good of those who love him, who have been called according to his purpose." Understand under your mess something beautiful is being created to do a perfect work living the life as a light to bring others from darkness. It's not about

Introduction

what man says about you; it's about what God says about you. God will use the lowest things on the earth to shame the so-called wise, and He has the final Word!

So no matter how bad things may look in the natural eyes of man, just know that God is working behind the scenes on your behalf. All things are possible with God on your side. The life we live on this earth isn't for ourselves, alone. We have a purpose. He has a greater purpose for us.

According to Jeremiah 29:11-12(NIV), "For I know the plans I have for you,' declares the Lord,' plans to prosper you and not harm you, plans to give you hope and a future. Then you will call on me and come and pray to me, and I will listen to you."

We need to prove that we are worthy of the calling that has been promised to us before the foundation of the world. Keep fighting the good fight because being in His Presence changes us. How great it is to know that we have a promising future after our testing.

It's comforting to realize that all of those past hurts truly did work out for our good. Every single wound that was opened will be cleaned and closed up one by one by our Father. He will use our hurt for His Divine purpose; nothing will stop God from fulfilling the purpose He has for your life. No devil in hell can stop us from reaching our full potential in Christ.

Being Freed From Darkness Poem

Understanding the ways the Lord is calling me to go; allowing self to be out the way.

Making room for His Spirit to move me in every area of my life; He is calling me to understand, that I've been set free from darkness and been brought into His marvelous light.

Since I'm in the light shining as the morning star everyone sees the star at night. So the people that are still living in darkness will see the star that shines forth to remind the people of the glorious things of our Creator.

He made the stars, sea creatures, and every moving thing on this earth. There is no way we can deny a Supreme Being even in the days of darkness.

Chapter 1

Childhood Crisis

Proverbs 22:6(KJV)
"Train up a child in the way he should go: and when he is old, he will not depart from it."

A child is a product of his environment; whatever is planted into that child is what is going to become of that child. If a child is raised in a household with parents who are abusive, negative, angry, miserable, depressed, unforgiving, and living in fear, those seeds are planted into that child. Parents are children's coaches. They are to teach children all the proper plays in life, so that they can be equipped for the game of the world; once it comes against them. If parents aren't equipped, due to a lack of training from their parents; they will need to go back into training.

If you play a game and you aren't properly trained to fight against the other team, you're going to lose that game. This is exactly what is happening to our children today. Our children are left ignorant, and without knowledge of who God is in their lives. They are also faced with a world that is full of un-forgiveness, pride, and jealousy. A world that is full of hatred, greed, envy, murder, strife, and division. We are losing our children to gang fights, to prostitution, drugs, and prison; they are being robbed of their freedom. The world is planting the seed in our children that chasing after the things in the world is going to make them complete.

Our children are looking for something, but that's the only seed being planted in them. The more they see these destructive things or hear about them, the more the worldly seed grows. Jesus says in John 10:10 (NIV), *"The thief comes only to steal and kill and destroy; I have come that they may have life, and have it to the full."*

Satan is the great deceiver, and he is out to deceive our children! Parents need to understand their role as parents and to know the importance of having a relationship with God. Not just knowing of God, but having a relationship with God makes a difference. When the parent(s) have a relationship with God it will show through their life style. The foundation of their lives should be built on Christ, not through the law to please the world. We have been given freedom in Christ.

Many parents do not even understand the importance of the role that they play in their children's future. Nor do they appreciate the special gift that God has entrusted in their care. Our children are very close to God, but under the wrong guidance they will become self-destructive. We have parents who treat their children as punching bags; which make the children think it is okay for them to get unloving treatment outside of their homes. Children start to believe it is normal to be called a b**** cause they grew up in a house being called that name more than their original name at birth.

In spite of how much love God has for our children, if parents are not demonstrating this love our children will feel unloved by other people. It will be hard for children to accept love from anyone else. Children begin to think it is okay to hate others due to the hate that is being shown to them. This may be the reason why children begin to get bullied in school, or become bullies. Children reflect the lack of love they receive towards others they come in contact with on a daily basis.

A child begins to build a wall to hide behind and conceal all the pain she or he is suffering. This wall causes the child to start feeling alone and unloved, rejected, abandoned, and unworthy with low self- esteem. All of these feelings may cause children to start acting out the pain they feel deep within.

Now the child is trying to fit in with others who are lost. The child is starting to do all types of things in order to feel accepted by others. Children will find themselves doing things that make them feel uncomfortable just to fit in with their peers. This may make children feel loved, temporarily, since that is what they are seeking. They are seeking a place to belong, inner worthiness, and other people to love them.

No child wants to feel unworthy or walk around full of hate. But if hatred is all that he has ever experienced, hatred is what he will produce. Parents must let their children know how much they are loved. Love is an action word. Parents need to speak and demonstrate love to their children, daily.

Children need to feel the authentic love of their parents. This is unconditional love which causes children to want spread a similar love to other people. Love overpowers hate, any time. Parents need to be more like Christ and teach children to spread love amongst one another.

"My people are destroyed from lack of knowledge." (Hosea 4:6)

I know the pain that many of these children suffer from because I've experienced it myself. I grew up in a household with both of my parents. My father was a truck driver and my mom was a stay-at-home mom. She did the best she could trying to manage a household of six children. My father was on the road most of the time as he tried to support a wife and six children. Due to stress, he became subjected to the familiar generational curse and began to create the exact foundation that his parents laid down for him.

It started with verbal abuse as my father planted negative seeds in his children, which made us feel unworthy, ugly, unloved and rejected as though we were never going to amount to anything in life. This escalated into being mentally and physically abused, which led some of us to drugs. Although my father provided for us financially, he didn't provide for his family mentally, spiritually, and physically.

My dad isn't a bad man. He just wasn't taught the proper lesson of life in being educated and spiritually equipped to raise his children to his full capability, which made coaching his home difficult for him. He just passed down the same seed that was planted in him. The seed that created him to be who he was; he was misguided.

I was mentally abused as a child; physically abused as a child; crushed in spirit as a child; molested as a child, and lost all confidence in myself as a child. My innocence was stripped from me as a child, which left me feeling abandoned and wary. I had lost my trust in other people.

Both of my parents had their own way of showing their love to me. It was love based on what they received as a child. My mother laid down the foundation of love and spirituality. Though she was uneducated, she planted the seed of forgiveness and genuine love toward others in me.

I learned things the hard way as a child because my parents never spoke about sex, diseases, or how to budget and handle finances, properly. My siblings and I didn't receive the proper tools we needed to go out into the world; Tools to keep the world from eating and spitting us out.

Due to the way my parents was raised it affected the way they raised me. I had two different seeds planted in me as a child: one from my mom and one from my dad. Both seeds were being watered, but the negative one my dad planted in me grew, rapidly. I started to believe all the things he ever called me. When others called me those same exact names, the bad seed was just being watered. It would only be a period of time before it started to eat away in me.

In our household we were always told children weren't allowed to speak. WE didn't have a place in the house to voice our opinions. If I voiced my opinion my parents considered it as being disrespectful. We were raised to never speak back to an adult.

Because I was trained not to express myself in any way to an adult, I became passive. This caused me to accept anything that came my way. It made me feel like my voice did not make a difference, or would not make a difference. It made me go along with a lot of things that I shouldn't have in my youth. There were so many things I didn't agree with doing, but I did them anyway. I felt like it didn't make a difference what I had to say, especially since children should never speak up at an adult, or question an adult's authority. This all stemmed from my upbringing as a child.

All the things that happened to me as a child started to form me as I became older. The father is the one who should demonstrate to his daughter what to accept and what not to accept from a man. The father is the first ministry experience a young girl receives. The father's behavior has a major impact on a developing young lady. If you are being slain by your own father as a young girl, this sets a model of the type of man you will become involved with as time goes on.

As a child, I was molested by my sister's boyfriend at the age of nine. My family really trusted this man. They never expected or thought this man could've or would've done such thing to me, and my niece who my parents raised. He did. I never told my parents or any adult of that matter. My niece and I kept that in for a long time. We lived in fear and never faced the problem. We were afraid of what would happen to us, if we told on that man.

That man is the father of my sister's children and somebody she loved. Who is going listen to us? We thought the best thing for us to do is stay quiet and bury that pain just like every other pain buried in me. That's another seed that has been planted in me allowing a man take advantage of me. I can love others, but I am not worthy enough to be loved back by others. I believed it was okay to be mistreated by men because my father didn't teach and protect me, better.

So a man my family trusted around my niece and I, molested us. He took complete advantage of our innocence. He was planting something in us; that we didn't realize was being planted. This seed was taking root inside of us for growth. The more we kept silent the more the secret ate away inside of us. That's why I always tried to protect my niece, because I know the pain that we endured together. My niece is like my sister, and I love her with everything in me. So from that day forth, I set my mind to protect her, always. I didn't care what anybody did to me as long as they didn't mess with my niece. Even, if it meant me getting hurt in the process. I felt like it was my responsibility to protect her from any danger no matter what it would be.

I have been wounded so much by people close to me, rejected and abandoned by people who say they love me. Beat down and wounded as a child by people trying to tell me what they think is best for me in my life. But all these people were doing was hindering me. I allowed people to put me in a box. It kept me from doing a lot of things I really wanted to accomplish.

Once I became a teenager, I rebelled. In middle school, I used to act out my pain in different ways. I used to try to fit in with everyone around me. I use to dance to inappropriate songs in the school hallways. I used to make myself seem tough when I was really weak and hurting inside. I didn't want anyone to see how much I was really hurting, so I built a wall to protect myself. I didn't trust people. I would only allow people to come so far, but I wouldn't allow them to enter into my heart. The ones who had my heart had already wounded me. So it was difficult for me to open up to anyone, else. My heart had now become completely harden due to the buried pain within me.

School was a struggle for me. I never had the encouragement at home, or support to meet my best potential in school. Since my parents were uneducated themselves, they weren't able to teach me anything I didn't know. So I just drifted through school as a person who was unable to truly focus on school. I was worried about how everyone was going perceive me. I didn't think I would be accepted by my peers, if they knew I needed help. So even though I needed assistance, I was ashamed to raise my hand to ask for help.

I was afraid of giving the wrong answers when the teacher tried to ask me questions, so I always tried to avoid being called. I thought I was a stupid child with no chance of getting anything right. My grades were not that great; I passed but it wasn't with me giving it my best. I just thought so low of myself that I didn't even give myself a chance. I always thought the worse about anything regarding me. Fear of what other people might feel about me kept me locked away.

High school was a totally different life than middle school. I tried even harder to fit in with everyone around me. My parents were extra strict; they never allowed me to stay over at anybody's house or go out. I was only allowed to go out with my parents or with certain family members. They wouldn't allow us to have any freedom. We had to stay close to them at all times. The only way I could hang out with my friends and have a social life was to sneak behind my parents' backs. My parents were so over-protective that I felt I had to sneak out to have any friends. Since my parents were so strict, I got involved in many different activities in school to try to gain freedom away from them.

Even though my parents weren't well educated they worked hard to keep us out of the projects. They always said how important it is to have education, but they didn't set an example for me of how to get educated. Children go by what they see, not what another person may tell them to do, especially if that person isn't practicing their own advice. The best way to teach a child is with your actions. Parents should always be mindful of the seeds they are planting into their children. Even though a parent with a bad habit might tell his child not to, in most cases the child will acquire the same bad habit modelled by his parent(s). It's true. Whatever you plant into your children will sprout up. I'm a living witness that the seeds planted in me sprouted in due season.

I started dating a boy in high school who I thought I really loved. He was my first everything. I gave my virginity to him, and he gave to me the worse reputation in the school. I was talked about and considered a freak amongst my peers because he told others about our sexual experience. He was the first person I had ever trusted enough to have sex. I was looking for love and I wanted to be loved. But I was also, suffering from insecurities, low self-esteem, and a lack of confidence in myself. This made me very vulnerable.

Things I always said I wouldn't do are the very things I found myself doing. I kept digging a deeper hole for myself to hide in due to my many wounds. I was in a lot of pain. Always trying to laugh things off or just trying to make other people feel good. I always wanted to make others feel good because of the pain I was suffering from within. I love to see people happy. I never wanted people to feel the pain that I was feeling. I kept falling in a deeper hole, and being buried under a lot of dirt. I felt alone like I was unable to talk to anyone. I didn't trust anybody, so I held everything in always acting like everything was okay with me.

I prayed constantly; I always had a relationship with God and wanted to do right, even at a young age. But I didn't listen to what God had to say to me because I was listening to everyone else.

I pray that parents really understand the everyday struggles children face, and stop taking their adult problems out on their children. The children didn't ask to be here; children have enough to deal with on a day to day basis. Parents need to be the strong towers children can run to in times of trouble; lending their ears to listen to their children's problems. Otherwise, their children might turn to all the wrong things and wrong people when they have problems.

At a young age I always tried to play peace maker, I knew how it felt living without peace within self. This made me want to be the peer mediator all the time amongst people. I knew what it felt like not being able to have anyone to speak to about things, so I wanted to be that person people were able to speak to if they didn't have anyone else to talk to. So they wouldn't have to experience the same pain I experienced in my life and go through life burdened with a lot of different problems. Allow children to know that you do care and that they are not alone. My prayer is that parents take the time to get to know their children and allow their children to know they are special. Raise them to know how much they are loved by God and their parents, too. And it is also important to let children know they are able to "achieve all things through Christ which strengthen them."

Challenge your children to meet their best potential. Be involved in your child's school work and communicate effectively with his teachers. Parents need to lay the foundation for the child. Allow your child to know the importance of having the Word of God rooted in their heart to teach your child the danger of living life without God. Keep them in the light so they won't fall into darkness. Speak truth to your children about generational curses that were brought upon the family. Explain to them that they have been set free by the Blood of Jesus Christ, so they won't listen to the lies of the enemy once he tries to approach them with the same stuff. Be honest with your children. Don't work so hard painting a picture as if you are the perfect parent(s). Always have that open relationship with your child, so they will know it's okay to keep trying even after making mistakes.

"Let us hear the conclusion of the whole matter: Fear God, and keep his commandments: for this is the whole duty of man." Ecclesiastes 12:13 (KJV)

"We know that the law is spiritual; but I am unspiritual, sold as a slave to sin. I do not understand what I do. For what I want to do I do not do, but what I hate I do. And if I do what I do not want to do, I agree that the law is good. As it is, it is no longer I myself who do it, but it is sin living in me. For I know the desire to do what is good, but I cannot carry it out." Romans 7:14-18 (NIV)

"Look straight ahead, and fix your eyes on what lies before you." Proverbs 4:25 (NLT)

Chapter 2

Teenage Pregnancy

At 16, I started to go to my cousin's house in Baltimore on the weekends. My parents never knew I had a boyfriend over at my cousin's house. I was busy trying to be loved by a boy thinking that was going make me feel better about myself. We started to have sex inside of my cousin's house every opportunity we had. We didn't use any protection and this young man was 18 at the time.

Then I started to skip school, so he could come to my house while my parents were working. He came by bus from Baltimore to see me. We use to spend the whole day together until it was time for me to get out of school. Then, I would walk back to the school, so it would seem like I'd been there the whole day.

One day while I was over at my cousin's house I started to feel really sick. Every time I ate, nothing would stay down, everything came up. I knew I had to be pregnant, but I didn't want to face it, so I kept going on with my life living in denial of the truth. The truth is very painful. I couldn't believe what was happening. I didn't want to face the fact that it was a major possibility of me carrying a child. Being pregnant is impossible. What am I going tell my parents?! I started to go through so many emotions. I knew I would have to face the truth soon.

One night my boyfriend called me at home, and told me that he had also been molested as a child by a man who was close to him. I couldn't deal with his revelation; I tried to make it work and be there for him. Unfortunately, knowing this information made me want to leave him alone. So I started to be real nasty to him. I told him not to contact me anymore as I didn't want anything to do with him. His situation just reminded me so much of my situation that I was running from. I couldn't face the truth about what had happened to me, and I didn't want to take on my boyfriend's baggage. Everything was getting out of control. I kept running from the truth. I didn't have anything else to do with that young man and I know I caused him a lot of pain.

As time went on another young man in school that I really had a crush on came to me and asked me out. He whispered in my ear, "May, I get your number?" I thought he was joking; this is the man that I'd wanted to talk to for a while! So I gave him my number, and we started to talk all night on the phone. I was still living life like I wasn't pregnant, yet the whole time I knew I was pregnant. I just didn't want to face the facts! So, I had this new boyfriend--- the one I always had a crush on. "I can't lose him," I thought. Things started to move along very fast with the young man and me.

We started to skip school all the time and were sexually active, as well. We never used any protection. I really was falling for this guy. So as my stomach started to become bigger I told him that I was pregnant. He never questioned if it was his baby or not. There were many times I tried to let him know it wasn't his child, but I was a young girl who didn't know any better. I acted in a very immature manner not thinking about the major consequences

Chapter 2 - Teenage Pregnancy

behind my choices. I allowed the young man to believe it was his child. I was hurting so much due to the mess I'd created out of my life.

Time went by rapidly. The young man came to all of my appointments. He stuck by me the whole time through the pregnancy. I really started to believe he was the father. Once you program your mind to believe something even if it is a lie you really start to believe your own lies. That is exactly what happened to me. I believed my own lies.

I had my first child at the age of 17. He was born June 18th on Father's Day. My boyfriend came to the hospital after I had the baby, and he was very excited about having a baby boy on Father's Day. He stayed at the hospital with me the whole time holding the baby, and talking with him. He was enjoying the moment of being the father of my baby boy.

Once I was released from the hospital, I went back home and discovered that my mother and her God-daughter had contacted my boyfriend to let him know that he might not be the father of the baby. I never knew this was taking place; they did this behind my back. I was so hurt. I really loved this man and didn't think he would want to be with me now because of what they told him. He was hurt. He called, asked questions, and broke up with me. He couldn't digest the information that was just given to him. I was very hurt. I believed it was the end of the world for me. We didn't talk for a while, but about a week later he contacted me and we got back together.

We both were excited to give things another shot. He treated our son well. He took good care of our son making sure he had everything that was needed. I loved the way he stood by my side, in spite of my mistake. We truly do love one another and he demonstrated unconditional love. This man showed me what unconditional love looks like in a difficult situation.

In 1999, I went back to school for a little while, but it started to be hard with a baby. So I dropped out of school in my senior year, not understanding the importance of having an education. I felt like I didn't need an education to make money or become a successful person. I figured I had it all mapped out how I was going do things. So I dropped out of school with a child. I asked my dad one evening if I was allowed to go out with my friends. He said he didn't care what I did since I didn't ask him when I got pregnant. I had hurt my father very deeply by becoming pregnant at such a young age, not having a means to raise my child, and then dropping out of school.

My father had always wanted the best for his children, and he wanted us to be better than him. He just didn't know how to express these things to us without being angry. I started to hang out. I was excited about gaining freedom--- in my mind I thought I've been locked up way too long. So I began going to the clubs, drinking, smoking cigarettes and stealing with my friends. I started to contaminate myself more and more with the things around me. I never wanted to do all the things I did, but I was hurting from the different situations that I put myself into. I wanted to suppress my pain, but I had more and more deep wounds developing over my body.

At 18, I became pregnant again with another child. Even though my boyfriend and I could barely support the first child, we brought another one into this world. I was working on different jobs and my boyfriend was doing what he could to help. We had

Chapter 2 - Teenage Pregnancy

our second son August 7th 2000. I had a stable job working at an assisted living home. We got a place in Freetown. I was always working while my boyfriend was home all the time with his friends, smoking weed, and hanging out in the house. I started to speak to him about this situation.

One day, one thing led to another and in his frustration at not being able to supply for his family like a responsible parent, he lashed out. In his insecurity, and low self-confidence, the seed that was planted in him at child hood sprouted into full bloom, and he beat up a woman in a stressful time. That's all he knew because he was a product of his environment.

From that day forth he started to become abusive. I never knew when he was going have a good day or bad day, but I knew that his moods could switch, quickly. I know it had to be a lot on him thinking about our first son not being his, and trying to raise a family with no money. He felt useless, as he watched his woman go to work, constantly, and manage the home. It doesn't make it right or justify him hitting me. The fact is a person only knows what they been taught and been around. The same way I know it wasn't right for me to do things either. Things were beginning to get way out of hand in Freetown with us, so he left to live in Pioneer City.

Shortly after that he became a barber. I left Freetown as well, and moved back with my parents. I was pregnant again with my third child. I let my boyfriend know I was pregnant. I told him I couldn't have any more kids. We are not keeping this baby, so I scheduled an appointment for something I am strongly against due to my belief in God. My friends and I went to the club on that

Friday night, and on the following Saturday morning we went straight to the abortion clinic.

While the lady was talking to me, I told her I couldn't do this and walked out of the clinic. On December 23rd my baby girl was born. She weighed only 5 pounds and two ounces. She was small due to all the toxins I was still putting into my body while being pregnant. I never stopped smoking. I thank God for His keeping power even in my mess. My daughter still came out healthy in spite of the blow I took in my stomach from my boyfriend while being pregnant. He didn't believe she was his child. He was frightened that the same thing that had happened with our first child was going to happen again. My boyfriend's friends were feeding him so many lies.

Still I continued to do the wrong things that could've caused harm to our baby girl. Inside I was going through so much. I thought I wasn't a good mother. I wanted the best for my children but I felt stuck in a certain position because I didn't get my High School diploma. All the wrong choices I made were catching up with me and driving me further and further into a hole. I just wanted to feel good and hide my pain. I was smoking quite frequently with my boyfriend. And it did take the pain away for that moment, but after the high went down I was still hurting. Every negative thing I ever heard about me kept being played over and over in my head. Even though I wanted to do right my pain was making it hard for me to do what was right.

I stayed away from my children for the whole weekend. I had to work every other weekend in a live-in position, so they could have the little that we did. It made me feel very low as a young mother, as a young lady, and as a person. I was working extra hard

Chapter 2 - Teenage Pregnancy

just to make ends meet. I wasn't happy with Natalie. I didn't like looking in the mirror or taking pictures of myself. I thought I was just a big messed-up person that didn't have any way out. I always prayed, and kept the bible close to me to read, but it just seem like I was going further into a pit. I wanted more for my children, but I wasn't able to provide the proper things for them. And I still had to deal with the desires and cravings of my flesh in this world.

The flesh is weak but the spirit is willing.

My boyfriend and I decided to move back with one another. I moved with him to Pioneer City. I was thinking and hoping things could be better for us. I knew he was a good person he just had some pain he was burying, as well. We had another son on October 7th 2003. After that child was born, I got my tubes tied. My boyfriend still didn't know how to control his anger, so it was the same thing over and over again. I wanted to leave so many times, but didn't have the courage to leave. I didn't consider myself worthy of any other treatment because I was used to being treated this way.

We moved from Pioneer City to Highland Village. Things really got worse once we moved out there. We were always fighting. I got tired and left him alone. God put the courage in me to leave him. Even though I loved this young man; I was only enabling him by staying with him. So I left it in the Lord's Hands and told God if it is meant for us be together He will bring us back together. Right now just wasn't the time. We started playing house at a young age without being properly equipped to handle the choices we made. Instead of enjoying our teenage years, we had to grow up too fast.

To all the teenagers out there, take my advice and reach out to someone who you can trust. Know that you are not alone, and spend time with the Lord. If your parents don't have a relationship with God make sure that you do. Get connected to a spiritual role model who really cares about what is best for you. Stay in school and get an education, boy-girl relationships can come later. Don't be deceived by the boys who speak sweet nothings in your ears, and mess up your whole reputation. Know your worth young ladies--- the Word of God states you are "beautifully, fearfully and wonderfully made," and you need to believe that for yourself.

You are precious in the eyesight of God no matter how anyone else views you. And you need to know your own worth… God has a lot of good things to say about you. Fix your eyes on what is right. Don't get sucked up in this world. The world has nothing to offer you but deceit. I don't regret having any of my children and I know God doesn't make mistakes. I can share my teenage story to help many other teenage mothers, and prevent children from making the same mistakes that I did.

Always apply yourself to whatever you want to become in life. Know that anything you really apply yourself to are the results you will receive. Be honest about your feelings towards things. Express yourself freely. It is not what you say, but how you say it. Show respect at all times and treat people the way you want to be treated. Live a life of love, peace, hope and joy.

"Do not love the world or anything in the world. If anyone loves the world the love for the Father is not in them. For everything in the world---the lust of the flesh, the lust of the eyes, and the pride of life--comes not from the father but from the world. The world and its desires pass away, but whoever does the will of God lives forever." 1John 2:15-17 (NIV)

Chapter 3

Self-Identity Crisis

Isaiah 59:1-4 (NIV)
"Surely the arm of the Lord is not too short to save, nor his ear too dull to hear. But your iniquities have separated you from your God; your sins have hidden his face from you, so that he will not hear. For your hands are stained with blood, your fingers with guilt. Your lips have spoken falsely, and your tongue mutters wicked things. No one calls for justice; no one pleads as case with integrity. They rely on empty arguments, they utter lies; they conceive trouble and give birth to evil."

Galatians 6:7-8
"Do not be deceived: God cannot be mocked. A man reaps what he sows. Whoever sows to please their flesh will reap destruction; whoever sows to please the spirit, from the Spirit will reap eternal life."

After my boyfriend and I separated, I struggled even more with self-identity problems. I didn't know who this person was that I'd become. I was just trying different things and wanted to fit in. I was on a road of loneliness, despair, debauchery, bitterness, vulnerability, low self- esteem, envy, idols, unforgiving heart, and mortal problems. I kept getting lost on this journey trying to find my way back. I kept taking all the wrong turns getting farther and farther away. I couldn't recognize myself. All I wanted was to find my way back on the proper road.

One of my close friends was a bisexual. One day I was over her house with another friend. This friend made a pass at me. We were a little drunk and acting crazy. So once the other friend left out of the room the friend proceeded with further attempts of touching me and I allowed it to proceed. I started to be caught up in that moment with that friend and continued messing around with her. I never had the intention or never wanted to mess with a female, but it happened that way. I always said that's something I would never do, but you never know what life is going to bring your way. I wasn't happy with doing what I was doing with her, either. It was becoming more than I had expected it to become.

There were plenty of times I wanted to just stop messing with this female, but she was so in love with me and she was a friend. I was caught up in a place of being ashamed of the person I had become. I didn't understand why I was allowing this to happen to me. Why didn't I just quit?

I started to dress in different clothing (at times as a male) just to make that person happy. I was always doing things to make others happy while I was in deep despair. I found myself in complete misery and distress. How could this be? How did I get on this road? I needed to find my way back. I didn't like this place. I was far from home, now.

I didn't enjoy being around that female in a sexual way. It made me feel very low and completely ashamed. In order for me to be around her, I always had to be high so I could suppress my true feelings. I hated the place I was in! I did so many things to cover up the truth of what was happening around me. There had

Chapter 3 - Self-Identity Crisis

to be another way. I couldn't continue on living this way; a change had to happen.

One day, I informed my friend that I couldn't do this anymore. I explained to her that I was getting back into the church, and getting things right with God. I just wasn't happy at all. I wanted more out of life. I was determined to find my way back on the right path.

As I started to get back into the church, I allowed the devil to have his way, again. I got involved with a married man at the church. There was something different about this man. We had become close, spiritually, but my intentions were never to get involved with him. He had a very powerful ministry. We started to work together.

One day he needed someone to speak with so, he asked if he could come over. I invited him over, and one thing led to another. The connection that he and I experienced was becoming very scary. We had gained a very close bond. I know the Lord had placed us in each other life for a reason, but we allowed our flesh to get the best of us.

We dated for a while. I felt so bad about messing around with a married man, but the feelings I had for him felt real. We studied the Word of God together and wanted to do right by God. The relationship we had was unbelievable! We didn't understand why we had such a powerful connection with one another the way we did. It was never about the intimacy. Our relationship scared us both! It was like we were one with one another, yet this couldn't be true because he is married to someone else. I knew the connection was only due to what we both were seeking after in a woman of God and a man of God.

I knew this had to end, but the only One that was going be able to end this between us was God. I had so many long talks with God as I prayed for His strength to work on my behalf. The Pastor and First Lady at the church tried talking to us, but we didn't listen. We knew how we felt about one another and the opinions of other people didn't matter to him. I always cared how people viewed me, so it bothered me how everyone spoke against us. I knew that I had to do what was right, in spite of my feelings. I also knew that it would take God to change this situation.

I didn't want to mess around with another woman's husband, but it happened. Oh, if people only knew how I felt about this situation! I was on a road that kept going in circles. Where was the way out of this place? God was the only way. I had taken the wrong turn on my trip trying to figure out who Natalie was. Natalie had been connected to so many people that helped formed her into all the things that she was currently in her life. Natalie was robbed of the glow that she once had. I felt that everyone in my life was contaminating me with poison.

Poison can either kill you slowly or rapidly depending on what type of poison you intake. I had put myself so far into the grave I didn't even recognize who I was anymore. I allowed everyone else to dictate who I was. I allowed circumstances to dictate who I was; I allowed the people in the church to dictate who I was.

If I had only listened to the Passenger who should've been the driver I wouldn't have taken the wrong turn. But I thought I knew it all. I heard the Passenger trying to guide me the right way, but I used the map in my head. So God allowed me to continue in my

Chapter 3 - Self-Identity Crisis

own strength; allowing me to believe that I really knew what I was doing until I realized that I'd taken the wrong turn.

That's the danger of bringing your GPS with you, but refusing to use it on your trip. GPS- Guider, Protector, Savior. In life we will go through various trials. Every decision we make will have a consequence behind it whether good or bad. There will be times when we will become discouraged. We will suffer from the lust of the flesh wanting the things in this life more than the True Living God. We start to allow these things to create us into the creatures that we have become on this journey to self- discovery.

We believe that material things and people will make us happy. We believe people need to give us credit before we recognize anything of value in ourselves. We believe we are unworthy, and we believe we are not able to have God act on our behalf like He did for others around us. We believe that our sin is too great for God to forgive us. We believe all these things about ourselves. All these experiences are part of our growing process. We have to go through some things in life in order for us to realize our true identity in Christ. God doesn't make any junk. We are beautifully, fearfully, and wonderfully made in His image.

We need to understand why we are on the road of self-discovery, and never lose hope. Always trust in God no matter what road you may end up on. Never be ashamed to speak to people about what you are going through. Never allow people to put their mess on you. Our lives were already planned out for us before the foundation of the world. In the beginning of creation we were living in darkness not seeing how sin would give us a sentence to death row. We thought our sin was hidden from the eye-sight of God, but it wasn't. Our sin can only be hidden from man. God sees all!

    The wages of sin is death. We are spiritually dead because of the various decisions we made as slaves to sin on our journey. If you are dead spiritually that means you are living your life in complete darkness. There is Life in Christ. Trust God even while you are living in the darkness; He can shine light on your situation, so you can find your way out of the dark road. Never give up, continue on the road until you find your way back on the proper path. Allow God to revive you in order to get back where He is calling you to go in life for His divine purpose.

Genesis 1: 1-2 (NIV)

"In the beginning God created the heavens and the earth. Now the earth was formless and empty, darkness was over the surface of the deep, and the spirit of God was hovering over the waters."

Chapter 4

The Idle Mind is the Devil's Playground

II Corinthians 10:3-6 (NIV)
"For though we live in the world, we do not wage war as the world does. The weapons we fight with are not weapons of the world. On the contrary, they have divine power to demolish strongholds. We demolish arguments and every pretension that sets itself up against the knowledge of God, and we take captive every thought to make it obedient to Christ. And we will be ready to punish every act of disobedience, once your obedience is complete."

Everything we do takes place by us thinking it first. So our thoughts have power over our behavior. You think something, believe what you're thinking and then you act off of what you believe. The mind is where the devil works best. The more you allow your thoughts to control you the more the devil is going to attack you by your thoughts.

Many of us base our life on a past moment, and then allow that circumstance to dictate the rest of our lives. It might have happened 5, 10, 15 years or more ago, but it still has complete power over you. For example, if your parents were always fighting because they never got along, you might have turned against marriage. You might have set your mind to never get married for fear of having a marriage like that of your parents.

Living your life in a box will deprive you of many things. Every day you should always ask yourself these questions: How are you occupying your mind? What does your day consist of you doing? What do you spend most of your time doing? What are your eyes fixed on? All these questions you need to ask yourself over and over again. Your eyes are the gateway to the heart. Whatever you have your eyes fixed on is what you're going to become.

Think about what type of seeds you are planting on a daily basis to be watered for growth, and whether they are positive seeds or negative seeds. Every day, we are planting some type of seed; whether it's a seed of negativity, such as: having an unforgiving heart, hatred, jealousy, bitterness, anxiety, sexual immorality, being a busybody, anger, homosexuality, or rebellious behavior.

I'm going speak a little about myself and how my thinking process kept carrying me further and further away from God. I had the seeds above planted inside of me, and they took complete control over my behavior. I didn't even realize I was being driven by my emotions due to these seeds. I didn't think I had any of those problems. Natalie was living life like she had it all together trying to mask every internal seed that was producing bad fruits. I always thought it was everyone else around me with the problem… not Natalie.

I was living my life in denial, and I never got to the root of the problem. I kept planting more seeds in bad soil, which kept producing bad fruits. I thought my body was the best thing on me, so I used that as an object. I never thought I was a beautiful person

Chapter 4 - The Idle Mind is the Devil's Playground

even when people told me. The seed was already planted in me that I was ugly from childhood. So when people always told me I was such a beautiful person, I thought it was just a lie. The only thing on me that I thought was fine was my body; so I started to flaunt it to tease boys, but wouldn't give it up to them.

I thought wearing sexy clothes revealing parts of my body was the way to go, and would get me the attention that I was seeking. I thought I was never going to amount to anything in life. Since I've been a child the seed was planted inside of me: "Natalie you're stupid; you're never going to amount to anything in life." I thought I would never be that mother, friend, woman, and wife, I know God has called me to be. These thoughts caused me to become very bitter. I see everyone else able to provide for their children; I see everyone else being happy. I see everyone else going through life with the best of both worlds. "What am I doing wrong?!" I thought.

I went into great despair. I found myself talking about other people that were doing well because I was so bitter. I became a busybody caught up in hurtful conversation about others. I began to hurt people with my words. I was giving back to them what was given to me. I would be quick to tell someone about themselves, but it was only because I was seeing myself through them. It is always easier to call somebody else out about the exact thing you know you have a problem with to avoid looking at yourself.

I thought my fleshly desires were too powerful for me to overcome, so I kept feeding that seed. I believed I was going be this way no matter what I did. So I started beating myself up about not being able to control the desires of my flesh. My flesh was completely weak, and feeding it what it desired didn't help the problem. I was my biggest enemy. I thought "My sins will never be forgiven and I am not worthy to be loved by anyone." How that thought caused me to do many things just to be loved and accepted by people.

My thoughts had me in prison for a long time. I had no way to escape the prison of the mind. I kept getting sentenced over again after I thought I reached bail to be released. I kept being convicted for the same crime. For example, if a person wants to change after being released from jail on bail... Why would they go back around the same exact people or things that caused them to be locked up in the first place? Especially, if they know they aren't strong enough yet, to go around those people. They have just set themselves up to go right back to prison because of their wrong choices after being released.

That's the way it was with me. Once I became a baby in accepting the Lord in my life, and trying to make changes for the better. I was still a baby in Christ... trying to play savior. I wasn't strong enough to go back around the same people who helped produce me into all the different creatures I have become; but in my mind I believed I was, and I was going to help them. Realistically, and spiritually there was no way I was prepared to go help anyone with the same problems I was trying to be healed from. If I haven't been healed myself; freed from my thoughts; and freed from the prison I was currently in... How could I possibly help another?

So I found myself gaining more charges after going back for sentencing than the charges I had before. My situation had become worse than it was before. My sentence was longer than it should've been because of the choices I made after my bail was

Chapter 4 - The Idle Mind is the Devil's Playground

set. I wanted to be released from the locked bars of my prison. My thoughts had such a stronghold over me that every time I tried to escape I got pulled back in. To escape I should have followed the Bible, the manual of Life that will give us the proper correction while in prison.

I was trying to get out before my sentence was over; trying find every easy way out so I wouldn't have to pay for the consequences behind my actions. I didn't want to spend that long sentence given by the judge after being indicted for the same charges over and over again. My thoughts drove me to spend plenty of long nights behind bars; and being in the dark made me lose hope. I couldn't see beyond what my eyes could see. What was in front of me was nothing but darkness with no sunshine.

"How good it would feel to have some daylight instead of being in darkness," I always thought. As I was in prison, I found a way to reduce my sentence. I started to read my bible more; I started to think positive thoughts; and I started to keep my mind occupied with the things of God. I started to be careful about who I allowed to be in my life; who was able to pour into my life; and who was able to be in my corner. All these things helped me to gain hope while I was locked up in prison.

The more I read my bible and prayed I started to see the light a little bit at a time. The more I saw the light start to shine the more I walked towards that light to see my way through this dark place. Natalie started to realize there is a better way on the other side of these bars. So even in my mess, I was preserved in order to get from these bars. I worked hard while I was in prison to become a better person and it helped build my character and the person I am today. I didn't allow my circumstances to stop me from seeing what God was doing in me, anymore. I started to realize that God sees all and knows all, so He sees what I don't see. After this I will be stronger than ever before, and won't have to return to prison for another sentence.

If I had gotten released from prison too soon I would've ended back up in the same place as before. There is a reason for everything. There is a time for everything. There is a time to mourn; a time to rejoice; a time of sorrow; a time of disappointment; a time of discouragement; a time of unbelief; a time of idolizing; and a time of pain, but just know through these times something new is going be born in you at the end of your sentence. You will be transformed into a beautiful diamond. The diamond has to go through a process before it becomes that shiny diamond in the store. All we see is how shiny the diamond is now on display, but not what that diamond had to go through in order to be placed on display.

Ladies, please understand that the bible speaks of us as being more precious than rubies. You don't have to settle for less because God has already spoken highly of you. Don't allow anyone to dictate who you are, or what you may become because of the time you had to spend in prison. Don't allow people to determine your future for you. Through your prison experience keep the faith. Don't lose hope. Know that God doesn't lie. Man may lie to you, but God can't and won't lie to you. Choose Life not death.

Women, you are more than your body, your clothes, your car, your fake weaves that you spend your rent money on to look good. You have inner beauty that you need to bring forth. Ladies, be aware, if you are ugly on the inside then it's going show from the outside. You don't need to live life like everyone else does.

Chapter 4 - The Idle Mind is the Devil's Playground

The same people that may seem happy are masking their misery. They're playing dress up, so you won't see their true image behind their make-up.

Don't allow your past failures to determine your future; we need to go through the struggle in order to be successful. If we never go through the struggle how would we learn to appreciate the life Christ has given us. He removed us from the age of darkness. No matter how long it may seem, please understand that God has not forgotten about you. Hold on to His promises and your reward will be great. Work hard to be who Christ called you to be; walking in His image, and not the image man has of you. God creates us to have Life more abundantly in Him; outside of Him is a life of hell. Don't be blinded by the things of this world, which kept us locked away for so long. But stand firm by the renewing of your mind.

Ephesians 2: 11-12 (NIV)

"Therefore, remember that formerly you who are Gentiles by birth and called 'uncircumcised' by those who call themselves 'the circumcision'(Which is done in the body by human hands)remember that at that time you were separate from Christ, excluded from citizenship in Israel and foreigners to the covenants of the promise, without hope and without God in the world."

Psalm 118:17 (NIV)

"I will not die but live, and will proclaim what the Lord has done."

Ephesians 4:29-32 (NIV)

"Do not let any unwholesome talk come out of your mouths, but only what is helpful for building others up according to their needs, that it may

benefit those who listen. And do not grieve the Holy Spirit of God, with whom you were sealed for the day of redemption. Get rid of all bitterness, rage, and anger, brawling, and slander, along with every form of malice. Be kind and compassionate to one another, forgiving each other, just as in Christ God forgave you."

Revelation 2:8-10(NIV)

"These are the words of him who is the first and the last, who died and came to life again... I know your afflictions and your poverty-yet you are rich! I know about the slander of those who say they are Jews and are not, but are a synagogue of Satan... Do not be afraid of what you are about to suffer... I tell you, the devil will put some of you in prison to test you, and you will suffer persecution for ten days. Be faithful, even to the point of death, and I will give you life as your victor's crown."

Proverbs 18:21(NIV)

"The tongue has power of life and death, and those who love it will eat its fruit. You can speak life with your tongue or curse God with your tongue. What comes out of your mouth is what makes you unclean because it is coming from the heart."

Matthew 12:34 (NIV)

"You brood of vipers, how can you who are evil say anything good? For the mouth speaks what the heart is full of."

How great it is to know this, with all the trouble we face...with people in the church degrading us, and shunning us for every mistake we made. People will always try to make you the talk of the

Chapter 4 - The Idle Mind is the Devil's Playground

day. They'd rather murder their brother or sister with their tongue. Look what the Word of God says about this. If you just hold on to faith while you are locked away going through your testing period; the great reward will be given to you. All of the people that the devil has put in place to kill you will actually be your stepping stool for success. This will cause you to gain victory over every situation; once you've been resurrected from the same thoughts, which because of your sin put you to death spiritually.

As I continued on my journey, I started to see the change in my children's father. He started to realize how much he needed me in his life (the same way I needed him in mine). So we talked about moving back together, and giving things another shot. At the time, I was living in Brooklyn located in Baltimore. He moved in with me. Our six months of separation showed us both a lot of things.

Things were going good with the both of us. Although, I still wasn't feeling so great about myself because of my deeply buried secrets. The young lady that I used to talk to was upset about us getting back together in Brooklyn. She was crying when she came to our house, one day. My boyfriend didn't understand why she was upset. When he finally figured it out; I denied the whole thing. I was too ashamed of my acts. I was still living in denial, and I couldn't admit to doing anything of that nature. I couldn't confess what I had done with that young lady.

I was just concerned about how I was going be viewed by people and my boyfriend. I didn't want to hurt him, and I didn't know what else to do. So I buried another seed within: I hurt a friend by denying everything that had happened. My life was in shambles, but I continued to press forward in spite of all the pain I was hiding.

All I wanted was to feel good and take my mind off the pain. I was so tired of the way I was living. I was tired of all the lies that I told to make myself look good, and protect other people from hurting. But all I did was make things worse. The people were still hurting, and most importantly, I was deeply hurt by the afflictions I caused other people.

Chapter 5

Fear

    Fear of other people's opinion of me had me wrapped up inside of a box not being able to breathe. I feared the unknown reaction of people, that is, if they would accept me after finding out the truth. Fear kept me in a place where life was being sucked out of me. I could no longer breathe. I was going through life as a zombie.

    I became numb to life. I couldn't feel anything any longer. I always wanted to become something great for my family, but being fearful stopped me. I was going through the motions each and every day. I felt like as an adult I still couldn't stand up for myself. I was fearful of speaking my mind to people because I never wanted to hurt others. I was always looking out for other people's feelings.

    I know this all stemmed from my childhood and the things I've experienced. I didn't want to see other people hurt by my actions; I was always trying to protect someone. My intentions were always good. But it doesn't mean it was the right way to do things. So many people were hurt by my decisions. "Hurt people, hurt people" is a very true saying.

    I never knew anything different than pain. I always internalized everything. Natalie couldn't speak the truth about her feelings. What did they matter anyway? The truth will only upset everyone else and hurt them. These are the things that kept running through my mind, so I kept quiet. The pain in me was running deeper and deeper. My whole life was full of pain.

All of my secrets were eating away at me and making me rotten. I was angry with myself because I would not stand up for myself. If you don't stand up for yourself no one else is going to take a stand for you. I was allowing people to run all over me. I became so bitter because of the things I allowed to happen. The only thing I had to do was open my mouth. I was frustrated with myself. Evil started to creep out of me. Different spirits started to operate in me. My thoughts were captivated by fear.

Fear was a very deadly medication for me. Fear controlled my every move. I feared: losing my boyfriend; allowing family to know how they had hurt me; allowing people to know what they have done to cause me pain; hurting other people; and becoming successful. I also feared letting people into my heart, and showing others the soft side of me. This medication killed the real Natalie.

I was later introduced to pain pills. One drug led to another drug. Weed, drink, cigarettes all go hand to hand with one another. Everything, I was doing just wasn't enough for me any longer. I needed something stronger to help numb my emotional pain. I was given Hydrocodone for the pain, I was actually having, physically.

As I continued to take the drug it was making me feel real good and taking my mind off of everything. I was so high off this pill. I loved the way the drug was making me feel. I became addicted because I always needed it in order to function or I would

Chapter 5 - Fear

feel angry. This was my HAPPY pill. I didn't want to be angry, and Hydrocodone made me happy for the moment.

I was taking these pills around the clock; every 4 hours was my self-prescription (as if I was the doctor!). I was living under the cloud, not wanting to deal with the real issues buried within me. In my mind, I thought I knew what was helping me face myself day to day. Many people today live their life based off of fear. This is such an unhealthy life style for anyone to live! This type of living caused me to be very unhealthy physically, mentally, spiritually and emotionally. I felt like I couldn't escape from this place. In spite of it all, I still kept pressing. Giving up is something, I never did even in my messed up state! I knew soon of later a breakthrough had to come.

Chapter 6

Drugs

As time went on I was introduced to more drugs: Morphine, muscle relaxers, Percocet, Lyrica, and any other drug that would make me feel good. I had to have these drugs, daily. I became a functional addict. I took these drugs around the clock. I mixed them all together which was very dangerous. It didn't matter I was already dead inside. I had placed myself in the grave. I was able to get my hand on these drugs any time I needed them.

I had a family member who had access to these drugs. I use to steal these drugs from her just to get a fix. I would never go steal drugs or money from strangers; I wasn't that bad off. I thank the Lord my boyfriend didn't even know I had a drug problem. I was able to hide it well. I was very functional while on the medications. I went to work high and went to bed high. It was just very simple to get my hand on these narcotics.

I use to fake being sick just to get my hands on these drugs. I always had something wrong with me. I use to travel from hospital to hospital, and doctor office to doctor office. Every time I went to get a fix, I was prescribed the drugs I wanted. The doctors always prescribed Percocet or Hydrocodone, and both of these drugs were fine with me. I made sure I went straight to the pharmacy to get the prescription filled. I didn't care how long I had to wait. I was patient to get these drugs that made me feel good.

Drugs helped me suppress everything that I had buried to continue going in life. I gained a sense of boldness; I started talking about my feelings to people. If I didn't like something I said I didn't like it, and that felt good. I was able to confront things that I wouldn't confront before without the drugs. In my mind, I thought Natalie was taking a stand, but it was only the drugs talking. The drugs had me in a totally different world.

Drugs didn't affect anything I did on a daily basis. I was able to do everything people asked me to do and my regular routine. I was doing it all with no disruptions. My work ethic didn't change or the heart I had towards people. I still always ministered to people. I just had a drug problem now. It was easier to do drugs instead of facing the truth about me.

I stayed on drugs for years without anyone even knowing I had a drug problem. I used to take drugs from the facility I worked at, as well. Drugs were always around me, and that was making my habit even easier to supply. There were times I wanted to stop, but it was making me feel so good. I found myself taking more and more drugs... chasing after my first high experience. I never caught it.

Deep down inside of me the real Natalie was screaming! I had covered her up with so much junk it was hard for her to find her way out. She needed to be released in order to see her true worth and break free. My own thoughts had damaged and carried me far away from home.

I believe this is what's taking place with people today. As I take a look around at people who are on pills; they are suffering from some type of trauma. They don't want to face the truth of

Chapter 6 - Drugs

their true feelings! They'd rather suppress the truth and live a false life! Living this type of life style only will bring more pain to your life. I know this for myself.

It's best to face the truth about yourself, and be set free from the things that are causing you to harm yourself! Understand we can cause more harm to ourselves by placing drugs into our system. The only thing that we are doing is running from our true self! Don't run any longer; walk into your deliverance to see the true you! The Lord will turn your ashes to beauty in due season!

Chapter 7

Marriage

At 25, I married the father of my children. We were still kids ourselves unstable starting a family of our own. We didn't even know the true meaning of marriage. We only went by what we seen and was brought up around. We both were brought up inside of broken homes being broken ourselves, having nothing to offer one another. The love we knew was love based on our own standards not based on the true foundation of God.

My boyfriend wasn't ready for marriage, and to be honest--- neither was I. I had joined a church, and knew that living together and having children without being married was sin. I told him it was time to make a choice: get married or separate. I was busy thinking about everyone's view of us and what the people in the church might say. All I cared about was walking down that aisle to exchange our wedding vows. He didn't really want to get married. He certainly wasn't ready to be the head of a household. We weren't equipped to raise a family. He chose to marry me, and at the time, I thought it was the right thing to do.

I didn't know the first thing about being a wife. Oh, I knew how to cook, clean, and work to provide for the family I'd created. I didn't know anything. I was a high school drop-out, and so was my husband. What were we going to do to raise our family? With no education, no career, no stability, no security or assurance…

what could we possibly offer one another? I was still on drugs not wanting to face all of the choices I've made in life. I felt as if I was at a dead end. Where else was there for me to go? I was still being controlled by my passions instead of the True Living God.

Love had blinded us to reality. We were living in a fantasy world, which we created for ourselves not realizing how all of our decisions were going affect our future and our children's lives. Where were all of the coaches to inform us of what would happen if we made the wrong plays in life? What were the end results going to be?

People always want to condemn you, and say what they think you should or shouldn't do. They may also advise you to not do something without providing a good explanation. Where are the people of the true Church who won't condemn you, but explain the truth to you in love and sound doctrine?

So many people fall into their own emotional doctrine, which causes the people of God to make wrong choices based on man's opinions. I think the emotional doctrine is the reason why the divorce rate is so high. Pastors and so-called priests are marrying people who they know aren't ready for marriage. They are encouraging people to get married according to man-made standards, instead of following the order of God-ordained marriage doctrine.

Marriage is a sacred covenant set up by God, not by man. Men use marriage to fill the void inside of their hearts. Anything you try to fill your heart with (instead of the true Living God) becomes an idol that you set to take God's place. God-ordained marriages are approved by the one and only God Himself. Any other covenant is nothing but a mockery of the True covenant, which God wants you to have with Him; once you allow His Will

Chapter 7 Marriage

to be accomplished in your life. But first, you must let go of your own will, which is driven by your fleshly desires and your pride.

Any false image (that you think is more important than God) is a mockery of what God can give you. That mockery will vanish. I made decisions based on emotions all of my life. I never made choices based on sound doctrine. I had placed many idols before God: drugs, cigarettes, friends, family, my job, my selfish ways, even church, and my husband. All these things I thought were more important than God. These idols were preventing me from becoming all that God had called me to be in Him.

I suffered from anxiety trying to do everything my own way in the world I had created. I believed I had the answers, so I wouldn't ask questions. I wouldn't allow anyone to try to tell me anything different, either. I was looking at everything through dark lenses. I stumbled a lot because I could not see anything clearly, yet this was not what God had created for me.

My husband and I struggled so much in our marriage. We tried hard to give our children the things they needed from us. It was so hard due to our financial limitations. I was the one who held a steady job with an income in the beginning of our marriage. My husband was in and out of jobs. He still tried to make sure he brought money into the house the best way he could. He did cut hair out of the house and found other places of employment. These were very hard times for us. We managed to always keep a smile on our faces, and despite of our trials we worked together. We both were very committed to each other and our family.

We were very stubborn people with much pride. We didn't know how to manage our finances; raise our children, properly, or even how to put our own wants to the side. We were stuck in the only lifestyle we knew. We never had any true stability in our household. Our children were missing out on a lot of things because of our lack of knowledge. We always had eviction notices on our doors, and we were evicted from a few places. We had to learn from our mistakes as time went on. Our life wasn't peaches and cream even though some may think it was.

Chapter 8

Being a Wife

It was so hard for me to manage my home properly as a wife and mother. I was suffering from so much pain. I needed deliverance from myself, so I could become the best wife God had called me to be. I needed to heal, so I could continue on this journey. I was under so much pressure as a wife and young mother. I was just trying to run the household, manage the children and make sure I stayed committed to my church, as well. I don't even know how I managed to do all the things I did. There were so many things on my plate. It had to have been the Lord's mercy. I give all the glory to the Lord!

I was very involved in my church. I went to church four days a week: Sunday, Tuesday, Wednesday and Friday. I was a very active member and one of the leaders, so the standards were set high for me. I didn't want to look bad and not be committed to my duties inside of the church. I attended church no matter what was going on with me or my family members. If I or my children were sick; we still went to church. Church was a must for me. Church was beginning to be before my family. I was living in this world like I was doing everything the right way. All I was doing was going by my own understanding of things. This world I created for myself and my view of life was completely false. Church shouldn't have been more important than my family. The Church is made up of family. The first ministry is the family. I had everything twisted. How had I allowed my own understanding of life to push me back so far?

I tried to make sure my family was fine. My husband wasn't involved in the church; he only came from time to time. I made sure my children and I stayed in the church. As a young wife I was very naïve. There was so much I needed to understand, but refused to get the help that I knew I needed. My pride wouldn't allow me to seek help. I always tried to cover up everything. I prayed constantly to God asking Him for help, daily. My heart was aching beyond measure. How can a heart be in so much pain? I couldn't see beyond my pain. Since I was hurting there was no way as a mother and wife I could lead my family, properly. It was really a hard time, and my hurt was over-powering me.

I had to look after my husband. He was always getting in some type of trouble. I felt like he was another one of my children. The people he hung out with were not the best influence. They weren't able to teach him how to be a man, or good father or better husband. It was like I was trying to raise a grown man all over again. I tried to keep him from making the wrong choices. I was beginning to act like his mother instead of his wife. My husband only wanted to do what he wanted to do. He always lied to me about every little thing. He didn't understand how to treat me as a wife, or act as a father. I always worried about him and that placed me under a lot of stress. I didn't think my husband understood the pain I was afflicted with already, and how much he added to that pain.

Chapter 8 - Being a Wife

The more I tried to control situations the worse things got for us as a family. I always wanted to keep my husband from making mistakes and I felt obligated to keep him from dangerous situations. Love isn't proud or boastful, love doesn't hurt, and love isn't controlling. I was trying to control everything to make sure our family was okay. Meanwhile I was drowning in my own pain. My husband still did what he wanted to do regardless of what I had to say about it. Once the law got involved it all fell on me to handle, anyway.

There were plenty of times that I sat outside of the detention center overnight waiting for my husband. I was so worried about him. I wanted to feel close to him and I wanted to be there once he was released. He was my responsibility, not anyone else's problem, so I did whatever I needed to do for him. I worked hard to make sure my husband didn't go without. When my husband was going through things I went through them, too. We were two young individuals learning about marriage through experience. We made plenty of mistakes, but we were always loyal to each other. As partners, we never turned our backs on each other, no matter what took place.

Chapter 9

The Rotten Wife

Everyone knows that something rotten leaves a bad odor. It stinks and the longer you leave that rotten thing around the stronger the smell becomes. That's how I was as a wife in the beginning of my marriage. All the junk I had buried within me left a bad odor. My unpleasant scent wasn't what people wanted to smell. I had a bad attitude, unforgiving heart, and selfish ambitions. I was full of anger, a backbiter, murderer, and liar. I was manipulative, controlling, jealous, bitter, and the list can go on. Everything about me was nasty. Even I didn't realize how nasty I really was back then.

I had a grudge against my husband. I acted out and rejected him sometimes because of his physical abuse towards me. No matter how much I tried, I couldn't forgive him for leaving me responsible for everything. I didn't like how he had treated me as his wife. I felt like he wasn't treating me any differently than the other men who had crossed my path. As you can see, I hadn't forgiven myself for my past yet, either.

Every time, I woke up in the morning to go work it made me sick. My stress level was on a high. My husband was in the house when I left for work and there when I came home, and I resented him for it. I knew as a wife, and mother I had to work, so my family could have food, transportation and a roof over their heads.

Only the vision God gave to me of us as a family encouraged me to continue on with my husband.

God gave me a vision of my husband and myself speaking to people to encourage them. The Lord also showed me the great leader that my husband was going to become. However, my husband didn't know the plans God had for his life. And even though I decided to stick with my husband the same way he stuck with me; it wasn't easy. I would always have the look of despise on my face when I came around him. Instead of encouraging my husband, I would always talk down to him.

I always manipulated situations to play with his mind. I would try to catch him in his lies. I never considered what he was going through, or how I might encourage him. Instead I accused him all the time, and tried to make him feel bad. I had a major issue with control. I could make him feel bad simply by using certain words, so he would give in to my selfish ways. I did whatever it took to get my way. I planted a lot of bad seeds, so focused was I on my wants. I didn't pay attention to how my actions had impacted his life.

The way I treated him made him feel worthless and like I didn't love him. Just because I was the only one bringing in the income didn't give me the right to treat my husband, badly. I treated him as though my feelings were the only things that mattered. My whole life thus far was based on my feelings. I was running off of my own personal feelings of things and not looking at what God was doing in the process. I was just basing everything on what I thought things should be like without taking my husband's feelings into account. I should've taken the time out to express myself, better.

Chapter 9 - The Rotten Wife

I was angry, frustrated, and without peace. I shouldn't have to come home to people in the house and everyone having a good time. Wasn't the man the one who should be getting out of bed every morning to go to work? Why was I the only one working? I felt used by him as though he just wanted me to take care of him. I didn't want my husband to even touch me. I didn't even want to be physical with him. I went through so many battles in my head about my husband's behavior. I always prayed to God for some type of break-through.

The saying, *"Hurt people, hurt people"* is correct. My husband was full of hurt as well, but my mind was on the hurt I was experiencing. I didn't want to treat my husband badly; I just did everything my way. I handled everything the way Natalie usually did, and no, it wasn't the right way. I held in every feeling I had against my husband, instead of us coming together and talking about our feelings. We never communicated our feelings. Everything was just internalized. My decision not to communicate hurt a lot of innocent people.

It was going take time to dig deep within myself and be honest with Natalie. It was going to take me to look past my own understanding to search for the inner truth. The inner truth is: Natalie is just a messed-up woman who never dealt with her feelings. She piled feeling upon feeling and acted out those feelings in a very negative way. It caused me to view all things in the wrong way. Instead of giving my husband the evil eye through his time of unemployment I should have been encouraging him. My life was just full of pain after pain after pain. All my wounds needed to be cleaned by God. A rotten wife is someone who is unhealthy to her husband. A wife should be able to nurse her husband back into good health. Any woman can walk around with a ring on her finger, but it takes a real woman to be a wife.

In the beginning of my marriage I wasn't a wife. Even though we walked down the aisle to exchange vows, I wasn't a wife. I was just another woman that had a ring on her finger not knowing the true value of her role. A true wife wouldn't degrade her husband. A true wife would respect her husband and his position as a man. A true wife would allow her husband to learn from his own mistakes, while being obedient instead of rebelling against him. A true wife would be at peace with her choices, and make sound decisions best for the whole family not just for herself. A true wife would uphold her husband, and trust his judgment even if she doesn't understand his choices. A true wife would trust God at work in her marriage and wouldn't trust in herself, alone. These are the things I didn't do in the beginning of my marriage. I had to learn these things through trial and error in real life experiences.

Trust was a major issue for me. Since I didn't trust people how could I truly trust God with my life, and better yet my marriage? I didn't trust my husband because of all the people who had hurt me in the past. I learned when I was young not to trust people, and that carried over into my adult life. I got married to my husband but I was scared to share my secrets with him. I didn't give him the ugly side of me. I wasn't going to trust him with my heart. Why should I trust him with my heart, so he could damage it like everyone else had? How could I always speak so highly of God but not trust Him with my own life and marriage? I always spoke to others about trusting God in their marriages and lives, but it was just hard for me to follow my own advice. There were so

Chapter 9 - The Rotten Wife

many things my husband didn't find out about me until later in our marriage.

Chapter 10

The Battered Wife

A woman that has been battered is very fragile and easily broken. She may have been misused by many in physical, mental, emotional and verbally abusive relationships. This type of woman is a very delicate package and needs to be handled with special care. She should have a warning sign on her that states "Fragile, item inside is easily damaged." Any time she is treated carelessly that sign is disregarded, and she will be damaged.

This is exactly what is taking place with our women, today. They are being handled the wrong way by the wrong people. They have been marked, hurt, and tampered with before meeting someone who would handle them with greater care. By the time they would meet a caring person, their package has been broken. These women may look pretty good on the outside, but soon their inner damage will spill out.

This battered woman is now also spiritually wounded, and needs to be nursed back to health. The old patterns that caused this woman to feel emotionally or physically inadequate in any way need to be changed. Patience is really needed when dealing with a battered woman. There are so many things this type of woman has been through. It will be a tough and on-going process to get a battered woman to see herself as the precious jewel she really is. It won't matter how many people tell this woman about that beauty she needs to believe it for herself. She has to feel her worth and true beauty that lies within her soul. And her future husband has been entrusted to handle her with the proper care she needs and deserves.

I was that battered wife. I truly understand what it is like to be misused by many. As a little girl I was always called out of my name by my dad. He never made me feel like daddy's special little girl. He disrespected me, degraded me, and beat me. So as a child I began to believe it was normal to be mentally, physical, verbally and spiritually abused. So in my own marriage I accepted this same type of behavior never understanding my true worth or the value of who I was as an individual. I allowed my husband to call me the b**** word; I'm saying allowed because I accepted this type of talk…he threw out that word so frequently. I was also physically abused by my husband in the beginning of our marriage.

My husband was full of anger, and he needed to know how to deal with the anger and stress within himself. He also needed male role models in his life that could teach him how to be a husband. The same way I needed female role models in my life to teach me how to be a wife. We both just needed the proper influences in our lives to help us along the way. He needed to be shown a new way of life and a new way of dealing with his anger. As I said before I'm not making any excuses for the reason my husband placed his hands on me or called me out my name.

As a battered woman, I had given power to those people who had hurt me. There was a man that I was trying to assist and encourage who took advantage of me. He expressed how he felt about me, but I told him we needed to do the right thing and not hinder one another's lives. We had met before without a problem,

Chapter 10 - The Battered Wife

and my intentions were never to be sexually active with this man. One day, I met with him, and he forced himself on me. He made me do things that I didn't want to do. I felt helpless, and I didn't know what to do. It caused me to believe that maybe I did something that encouraged him. I was so naïve. How could this be? And how did I allow this thing to happen? I didn't tell anyone that I was basically raped by this man.

Even after he raped me, I didn't turn my back on this person. My heart was full of more pain trying figure out how could this be? I believe I was more in shock and couldn't even process what had taken place. I finally told my husband that I was raped. He never even responded to me. It seemed as if he didn't care. I felt as if what happens to me just didn't matter. I didn't even feel loved by my husband. I had told him I was raped, and he didn't say anything. My husband's lack of a response impacted me, as well. I didn't want to face the fact that I was raped. That is really hard to digest and admit to yourself. Once again I've been violated, and misused by someone to whom I tried to show kindness.

The Word of God states "The people perish for the lack of knowledge." God was showing all the warning signs to me, but I didn't pay attention. I kept thinking I could help people and save them from their messed-up state. That is so comical coming from a person that still needed to be saved from her own messed-up mindset. God didn't want me to allow these individuals to trap me into falling victim under the enemy's control. But, I'm the type of person who has such a big heart that likes to give people the benefit of the doubt. I love to help people, and I always look for the good in people instead of the worse. It was just so hard for me to break free from those old mindsets. Every time I thought things were becoming better, the enemy took me back to a certain place in the mind that I didn't want to re-visit.

Many people wonder how a battered woman can continue to live in the same state. It's easy, and you won't know unless you've walked in a battered woman's shoes. I had become accustomed to this life style. I didn't know anything different. All I knew was the life that I kept repeating over and over again. It all became a cycle for me. I couldn't see past this state that I was in at the moment. I kept making myself believe that I was fine. The truth of the matter was Natalie needed some healing and a way out of this mindset. This is not the life I want for myself. This is not the life style I'm trying to keep repeating over and over again. I need a renewing of the mind.

It's time for me to be washed clean of those thoughts that kept me living the life of a woman without any hope. It is time for Natalie to stop playing victim. A victim is always pointing fingers, playing the blame game while living a hopeless life. That is not the life style I'm going to choose for myself. I will no longer be stuck in that kind of life style; because it has prevented me from living on the new level God has ordained for me to live in Him. I have become a survivor, which means I need to live as a woman who has survived this condition; instead of a woman who can't make it out of this condition. There is a big difference in being a woman who is a survivor. A survivor learns from their experiences and is victorious. A survivor celebrates all of the challenges she has overcome.

I will take a stand and not be walked all over like a carpet. My voice will make a difference; save many other people for living unhealthy lives, and help them to make better choices.

Chapter 11

Walking into My Healing

Scripture on Forgiveness:
Matthew 11:28-30
"Come to me, all who labor and are heavy laden, and I will give you rest. Take my yoke upon you, and learn from me, for I am gentle and lowly in heart, and you will find rest for your souls. For my yoke is easy, and my burden is light."

In order to walk into my healing, I had to start forgiving whoever had caused me pain in my life. This was not an easy process. All the things that I had ever covered up had to be exposed in order for me to receive my healing. I had to forgive every person and forget about the pain buried so deep within me. God began to show my hardened heart to me. I didn't realize how hard my heart had become. I had become so accustomed to just pretending nothing mattered that I was numb to the truth. It was much easier for me to pretend everything was fine instead of facing the reality.

God also revealed everyone I never forgave for cursing my life. He wanted to free me from the negative thoughts of their words and actions against me. I wondered why I kept going in circles and behaving badly. I didn't realize how my negative thoughts were holding me back, and causing more pain in my life.

I had to begin forgiving everyone whoever hurt me so I could become free! This was hard for me to do, but necessary in order to move forward.

I reached out to each person by phone. Using Facebook, I contacted the man who molested me as a child to let him know that I forgave him. I genuinely have forgiven him, and I am able to hold a face to face conversation with him, today. Forgiving him took a lot of negative weight and stress off of me. The Lord gave me enough wisdom and revelation to realize this man never wanted to do these things himself. The man was affected by a generational curse that is covered up or whispered about in a lot of families. He might have also suffered similar abuse in his childhood. I begin to feel compassion for him and others in his situation. Many times in life as we allow other people to know we forgive them...it can set them free from guilt, too. Guilt can kill you slowly! I think that is the truth God wanted me to see.

The next person, I spoke with was my dad to inform him of all the pain he caused me by his words. His words were a curse over my life. Now, I know my dad meant well, but that was his way of communicating his love. It didn't make it right, but that is all he knew. Today my daddy and I have the best relationship. I even told my dad how much I appreciated all he did for us as children. My dad worked hard to take care of his family. The more I forgave and spoke out about my feelings and my thoughts; the freer I became.

The next person I had to speak to was my husband. I had to let him know how he had contributed to my pain, and that I forgave him for all the things from the past. He had to know how what we had been through had hurt and affected me as a woman.

Chapter 11 - Walking into My Healing

It felt so good to finally release all of those piled up feelings to my husband. Finally, I was being honest with myself! Everyone needs to know their feelings do matter and need to be communicated to one another. We all need to talk, otherwise miscommunication, or lack of communication will cause problems between people and in relationships.

Chapter 12

Forgiving

There are so many mistakes that I made due to my mental state. I felt so guilty about all of my actions. Once, I had asked God for forgiveness, I learned to forgive myself. I made sure I told my husband everything about me that he didn't know. I had to be honest with him! I never allowed my husband to enter my heart because of my bad experiences. I didn't think my husband was going to accept me, so I had to hold up to a certain standard even if it was a lie. In order for me to rebuild a healthy relationship with my husband, I had to reveal my secrets. God was restoring everything in my life to walk in my healing! By His stripes I am healed.

My husband and I have the best relationship now. He treats me like his Queen and I treat him like the King he is to me! He understands now how it feels to be showered with genuine love! We communicate daily about our feelings and don't hold anything back from one another. We speak truth in love! We are best friends, lovers and life partners! A change has come over me that is truly impacting my whole family! Natalie is being set free from her own way of thinking. I'm now operating in sound doctrine and seeking the wisdom of God. I thank the Lord for restoration!!

My husband understands our past is our past and my feelings were just feelings. Our love for one another is deeper than ever before. People may not understand our story or how we as a couple do things, but what matters is the understanding we have about one another! God knew which type of man I needed in my life to help heal my heart and continue on this journey called life. God also knew the type of wife my husband needed with him by his side! We just had to grow up to be the man and woman God has called us to be for one another!

Growing up is never easy or fun, but it's required in order for people to move into the next level of their lives. Many people would rather not grow up, and they are comfortable in that state. I just couldn't be that way for my family or my husband! We have the best years ahead of us in our marriage. We may have been through a lot in the beginning, but we are stronger as a unit, wiser, and understand more how a marriage is supposed to be. We have goals and are working together to create a better life for our family to get out of our current situations because of our past mistakes. Communication is what we do best now, and that keeps our relationship healthy!

Relationships are ruined through miscommunication. I thank the Lord for loving me enough to break me down to see me. I took ownership of everything I've ever done to other people and asked those people for forgiveness. The process truly helped me to confront all of the issues in my life that I've always avoided. I had to go through this process to live the life God has ordained for me. Now every relationship that was unhealthy is being rebuilt to be healthy. I couldn't run any more from the truth…The truth was always hitting me in the face. I'd rather hear the hard truth instead of lies. I lived a life full of lies and secrets long enough. I want to continue to be free and be real about my feelings, and

Chapter 12 - Forgiving

honest about my hurts. Sparing my feelings will only cause more pain. I now chase after the truth instead of running from it.

Chapter 13

Deliverance

The Lord had to bring me to a place by myself, so I could become free from myself and current condition. The more I forgave and asked others for forgiveness and faced the truth, the more I've became free from all of the drugs! God took away the desire for the different pills I had been using to suppress my true feelings. Smoking weed and cigarettes was taken away from me, too! The more I walked in the truth the more things were coming off of me that wasn't of God. I was freed from every spirit that held me hostage! Those spirits had kept me in the dark for so long. I couldn't see the light, but when the Lord shined His Light in my life a sudden change came over me. The power of God is being manifested inside of my life, now.

I was transformed into a new creature. My old ways had fallen off of me and I was just hungry for the Word of God. I received divine healing and intervention from God, my Father Himself, not a physical healing from the doctor! God was the only person that could save me. He stepped into my life just in time because God knew I needed the Savior to deliver me from these spirits. Natalie would probably be dead if God hadn't intervened. I remember being hooked on all of the different medications, and I had a dream of my own death! In a vision, I had a heart attack, and I heard the Lord warning me very clearly to stop using drugs. The vision felt so real at times, I even felt my breathing stop during my sleep. When God stepped in to lead me out of the darkness, He showed how much deliverance I really needed. I am forever grateful, and I now empathize with other individuals who are walking the path from which the Lord delivered me.

God can use you to help others get delivered from what He released you from. Remember God didn't deliver you from these spirits for yourself only. You were delivered to help another soul get freed. It's time for us to walk together in unity to help each other along the way. People are always so quick to judge what they don't understand. That is exactly why so many people are walking around hurt and abused.

I know what it's like to be misjudged and misunderstood by people. Everyone always have something to say, but don't see themselves. It's much easier to judge the next individual instead of looking at self. Only when people would truly examined themselves are they able to focus on their own problems… instead of trying to put down the next person to make themselves feel and look good. Life is not about who you can tear down; it's about who you can build up.

Instead of talking about another person, and forgetting where you came from, pray for or with that person. Share your story with the next person. You'll be amazed how your story can help someone else to be set free! I thank the Lord for setting me free from worrying about how people will perceive me. If I was still in that state of mindset I'd be in complete bondage and wouldn't be sharing my story now. My passion is to save as many people as I can. Of course everyone won't be saved, but I will work hard to help as many people who are willing to be helped. I will fight for people

Chapter 13 - Deliverance

to be set free and delivered the same way God set me free. It's time to break free from the prison of the mind and walk into the life that has been ordained for you.

No longer will I allow people's opinions to stop me from walking in my deliverance. I will take a stand and operate in the strength the Lord has bestowed upon me to carry out my calling. People can say what they like, but one thing they can't say is Natalie isn't transparent and stuck in bondage. Always remember the same people that are talking about you wish they were bold enough to speak out. They are just living a fearful life being controlled by other people's opinions of them! Be different and apart from the things that seem normal in the eyes of the people around you. Be bold and courageous in receiving your deliverance! I refuse to be like the next individual. I will be successful and walk upright being humble and loving to my enemies! Love covers a multitude of sin and can deliver people around you. Don't allow anyone to stop you from receiving what God has for your life. God created you for His divine purpose!

Breaking strongholds over your life is hard, but it will become easier with the Lord's guidance. Everything must be taken to the Lord in prayer! This is a spiritual battle not a physical battle. The enemy is out to kill, steal and destroy the things that our Father has promised us since the foundation of the world. So in order to break from these strongholds you need to examine your thought pattern. If your thoughts don't line up with the Word of God then those thoughts must be plucked out of your thought pattern. I have a remedy that is applied to my life. It allows you to examine your moods and whatever is causing the change in your moods. We all know that our thoughts control our behavior. If you wake up feeling a certain way or start feeling a certain way through the day it's due to your thoughts.

I've applied the following procedure in my life as a remedy for correcting my thought pattern using the colors of the traffic light signal. A red light means "STOP and think" about thoughts that arise; a yellow light means "WRITE IT DOWN"; and a green light means "GO TO THE WORD OF GOD." If your thought doesn't line up with the Word of God; it's not from God. Pluck that thought out of your memory bank. It needs be uprooted and replaced with a positive Godly thought. Bad thoughts need be destroyed from your life to fully walk in your deliverance. Don't allow your thoughts to continue having power over you. Start to follow this procedure to gain control of your thoughts. It truly does work!

Your thoughts have the power to create your reality! Your world is created by your thoughts! That's why renewing of the mind is so important, which come from the strongholds being destroyed from your life. The light and darkness have no association with one another. Living in the darkness comes from your own reality created through your own thoughts. The light comes in to lead you away from the darkness destroying those chains! It's our choice to walk in the light or stay in the darkness! God won't force Himself on us! It's our choice to choose either life or death! I chose to live a life full of life!!! Walking in the light operating in spirit and truth! Death is anything contrary to the Word of God in your life; on this day you must choose what you are going to believe! Walking in the light is walking in the Spirit which is the Word of God operating in the truth! Greater is He within you than he that is in the world!

Chapter 13 - Deliverance

A short testimony on my thoughts: My thoughts had me living in a world which was completely delusional! I was so fearful over the smallest things in life. I suffered from anxiety when I felt like I didn't have any control. It seemed like it was the end of the world for me. It took me into a state of depression. I believed Natalie had to have control over everything in order for it to go the proper way, that sounds crazy right?!?! How could I have possibly believed I had the power to control everything around me or what takes place in my life?!?! I don't have that type of power. I am not God! You see how the enemy can easily plant these thoughts and we start to feed off of these same exact thoughts?

I never had the proper peace to be able to operate in a sound mind! How, could I… if everything caused me to have anxiety? Now I thank the Lord for allowing me to have His peace which surpasses all understanding in chaotic moments! When the storms of life are raging around me, I have peace…because I am trusting God in spite of what I see. He allows me to see how He is able to handle things way better than I ever could handle them! Deliverance….Again it took God to intervene on my behalf in order for me to be delivered from my fearful mindset, which caused me to be very delusional! Don't get me wrong, this certainly was not easy and still is not easy. The more, I relinquished control the more things worked out in my favor.

This doesn't mean that whatever you believe should take place for your life will happen. This means that control has been relinquished to God for His Will to take place in your life. Sometimes you won't understand God's Will, and you might want to turn back. God's Will is better for our lives. Look how we have already messed things up by doing things our own way! For a time, many things we don't understand and find hard to accept will take place. People and things may be purged from our lives; we have to be open to changes in order to evolve. The one thing we must remember is: accepting this process is for our own good! God's plan for our life is the most important thing for us to do! It will lead us to a life full of milk and honey and proper connections to help us along the way!

 I know for me it was hard to accept this process in the beginning. I'm very analytical which doesn't always work in my favor. I would try to figure out all of the moves in advance that God would show me. It's so funny now as I think about all of this. I would dissect everything placed before me trying to get my human mind to comprehend God's plan! It was like solving a puzzle… I would spend so much time trying to solve that one puzzle and putting the pieces in the wrong places. This would cause me to miss what God was truly doing or saying to me. As the Word of God states, "His ways are not our ways and thoughts are not our thoughts!" So why was I trying to figure out God's thoughts?! So many times… I looked for God to do something in one way believing I had it all figured out and to my surprise He did it in a total different way! God is so amazing and has our best interest at heart. In spite of our mess God is always by our side waiting on us to surrender to Him.

 Something I needed to learn was God can make a way out of no way. All things are working for your good according to God's purpose for your life. The Word of God states "life and death is in the power of the tongue." The more you speak life over yourself

Chapter 13 - Deliverance

and your family the more you will shift the atmosphere around you. Your words will cause things to change around you! Your words can bring deliverance into your household or curse your household. Everything you've been through will not be wasted it's going to help deliver another soul from their messed up state!

It's so true how God will use that thing which held you in bondage to set another person free or break a curse in your family's blood line. Your past bondage will help you to be motivated to make a difference in your own family, so chains will be broken. The curse will end and leave your blood line. I know that my bondage experience helped to deliver me from cursing my own children and planting negative seeds in their lives. God taught me to use wisdom in my words when it came to my children. I teach my children to never speak negative words over themselves, siblings, friends, family, their parents, or anyone. They are taught every time a word is spoken it's a seed being planted for growth. So I teach my children to carefully choose their words. I know how words have damaged me, and how long it took for me to be healed from them. Where much is given much is required…if you have been forgiven of much and delivered from much that exact thing needs to be instilled into another person.

We are required to give back the gift that God has given to us to other people, now that we are delivered and free. Many people are yearning for truth, and looking for someone they can trust to help them along the way. Our life style is what people are watching; it speaks high volume. People are tired of lies after lies! People have become so accustomed to believing the lie is a truth that the truth is no longer recognized or accepted! How backwards is that? The people in this world need to be awakened from out of their deep sleep and stop living their life like zombies. It's time to face the things deep-rooted within in order for you to walk in your deliverance. Deliverance......Deliverance......Deliverance….. WALK IN YOUR DELIVERANCE….It's time for the chains to be broken off of your life and your loved ones, too!! Take baby-steps into your HEALING!

Chapter 14

Connections

It is important for you to understand that who you are connected to makes a major impact on your life. For an example, if you don't have your lamp plugged into the socket….when you hit the switch the light won't come on. Believe it or not that's how it is with the people in our lives. If we are connected to negative people in return there will be no light. The only source we'll get in return is complete darkness. Remember, "negativity + negativity = Negativity source of energy! This will drain the life from out of you. Being connected to the wrong people is like dragging dead weight that slows you down. You need to break free from this type of people.

The only thing negative people want to do is discourage you; they are joy suckers! The more you try to speak life they will trample all over your dreams! These are the type of people you don't need in your corner. They are small-minded people who can't see past their own pain inside of their lives. Since they can't see past their own pain and they don't believe in themselves; they want you to join them in their misery! Misery loves company! If you want to grow that means a separation need take place. There is no way you can walk into your healing, living a life of purpose being connected to these type of people.

So a disconnection will take place. God will begin to shift some things in order for the light to come through in your life. Certain people who are hindering your life will begin to be removed and new people will take their place. Don't fight this process, you don't want to hold on to anything that's preventing you from moving in the next level God has ordained for your life. The hardest part is when you get disconnected from childhood friends, and family. This process is very painful, but must occur in your life. You can't take everyone with you on this journey! Some people must be left behind. A change must happen…so disconnecting yourself from things that don't mean you well is very important! This even includes being connected to the proper leadership.

If you aren't connected to the proper leadership you will be led astray! Since everything starts with the head, if the head is lacking confidence, trust, faith, love, knowledge, wisdom, love for people, or is very prideful; these are the traits you will lack, too. Whoever you are connected too must be able to bring life into your life. You should be able to learn from these people. These people should have your best interest and heart. These people should pray with you or for you. These people should be very genuine. These people should speak truth to you and not worry about your feelings, but be more concerned about your well- being. It's so hard to find people like this in today's society, so when you do, hold on to them. Even inside of the church and your church supposed to be our safe haven!

Chapter 14 - Connections

I know for myself as God was transforming me more and more into his image many people were removed from my life. God had to place people in my life that could really bring and speak life over me. I was so tired from always pouring into everyone else. I was always giving and never getting back. I felt used, abused, and unappreciated! God knew I wanted a change...so he allowed a change to take place. Every person that sucked the life from me was removed! Every person that always had something negative to say due to their lack of knowledge was removed from my life. Every snake in the grass God has exposed to me. It hurt me to see the truth and be separated from these people, but it was necessary.

If I wasn't separated from these people...I would've never been able to find myself in Christ. I would have been trying to still be all the things people thought I should've been in their eyes. The wrong people pouring into my life had caused me to become discouraged from my ministry. The ministry... I know God had called me to as a little girl. I began to doubt my gift and calling in Christ. I started to sway away from the things I had a passion for. I made myself believe that maybe this just isn't for me anymore and I had heard God wrong. This process occurred with me because of all of the conflicting thoughts of the people around me. I truly doubted my ministry! Lord thank you for leading me and bringing the right people into my life! My whole family would've been destroyed! My God, You have been with me the whole time!!! Oh how I thank You for Your keeping Power!

When, I think about all of the things that could've occurred in my life; Your love for me is unexplainable! The enemy was out to kill me through people, but You blocked it, Father! I have to take a minute to give You a praise break! Oh how worthy is Your Name!! The KING OF KINGS, LORD OF LORDS! You are the great I AM! How magnificent is Your Name! I thank You for my husband and how You have touched him in a mighty way! I thank You for continuing to open his heart, and giving him the proper people in his life! You knew all things, Father, before they occurred since the foundation of the earth! Words can't express my gratitude towards You! I thank You for restoring my family back to good health! What would I do without You, oh Lord?!? I thank You for setting me apart to live a life of love, peace, everlasting joy, happiness and self-reflection! Always looking in a mirror at myself instead of bringing down another soul! In Jesus' precious Name! AMEN....AMEN...AMEN!

I had to take the moment out to praise my Father above! As I was typing I begin to think about His goodness! I thought about every person He removed from my life and the blessings He bestowed upon my life. God has placed some wonderful humble people in my life throughout my journey to help me along the way. At each level He promoted me to He made sure my needs were supplied! Who can't give a God like that some praise?!? All because of His love for me! Every positive person who poured into my life helped form me into the person I am today. I even thank all of the negative people that helped me, too!

Right now God has connected me to the Palmers; they are the lead Pastors at Kingdom Celebration Center church...where we "Love God, Love People and Fulfill Needs!" God placed them in my life during a very rough time for me. I was broken in pieces so I could be remolded. This ministry truly impacted my life in a major way! They nursed me back to health and spiritually I was

Chapter 14 - Connections

revived! I was resurrected from the dead! Everything I have a passion in doing is provided in this ministry! It's so amazing how God has your whole life planned out for you, but you must walk in the ways He is calling you to go! That means being obedient is very important on this journey! This ministry taught me so many things and opened my eyes to see things in a different perspective. The teachings provided here are out of this world! I see exactly why God brought me to this ministry! This ministry teaches in Greek, too!!! My passion is to learn Greek and other languages!

I'm truly able to learn from the Palmers! They are humble people who have the heart to help people around them. They are entrepreneurs who are working hard to provide jobs for the people in Anne Arundel County!! I love the Palmers not just for what they have done for my family, but for who they are in Christ! They are great leaders in the Kingdom of the Lord! That's why being connected to the right people is very important. <u>You are what you eat, but you can't put everything into your body!</u> You have to be sure you are eating spiritual food from the Lord's Table.

Chapter 15

Obedience

The Word of God states "obedience is better than sacrifice." Obedience is surrendering to God's plan for your life and letting go of your own will! I said "Okay Lord, I trust you with my life; I want to do your will!" Yet, His Will didn't make sense because I couldn't understand it, so I began to do things my way… again. The Lord always made it clear what He wanted me to do; I just turned a deaf ear like I didn't hear Him speaking. I have always found it difficult to be obedient. I'm not proud of this, but the truth is I'm very stubborn! My stubbornness prevented me from being obedient when I received assignments from God! I had issues with the people in the assignments. I found myself questioning God, and asking Him "Why me?"!

I had to learn to hear God's Voice and obey His Voice once He spoke to me. God made it clear to me that these people's blood are on my hands, so not being obedient to Him could destroy another person's life. I realize it's not about Natalie; it's about God's purpose for His people. God sends people to help as an answered prayer to another. I had to learn this and follow every instruction given to me by God! Behind every instruction is a blessing! I was chosen for His divine purpose! I had to stop arguing and accept the calling God placed on my life! When we learn to be obedient to God (despite our own feelings) things will be much better for our lives.

In many cases my family had to pay for my disobedience! I even had to pay for my disobedience! When God has a call on your life there is no escaping it. I had to walk in my calling which is a part of my healing… accepting what God has for me. Now I am more than willing to follow the instructions God gives to me. That doesn't mean it's easy, but I must follow His Will for my life! OBEDIENCE…..OBEDIENCE….OBEDIENCE… It's so awesome to know how God is always with us! He will never leave us nor forsake us! Even when we leave Him, He still waits patiently for our return! He doesn't just give up on us like people do! He is always present! Being obedient to God is a sign of being humble, grateful, reverent, respectful, submissive, listening to His instructions, and surrendering to His Will. If you aren't doing any of these things, there is no way you can tell me you are being obedient to God! Not the True Living God!

Chapter 16

In Closing

In closing, if you don't take anything else away from this book... Find out who you are in Christ! Dig deep within yourself and see what is preventing you from moving forward in life. Be honest with yourself and stay connected to people who can keep you accountable. Seek out God's purpose for your life and pray to Him daily for your healing! We all need to be healed from various things that occurred in our lives. See what you need to be healed from in your life! Begin forgiving people who caused you pain. This is not for those people, but for you to regain your power! The more things you hold against an individual gives that person power over you! It's time to get your power back!

We must diligently seek out God's plan for our lives, daily. Read His Word on a daily basis and ask Him for revelation for your life. Live a peaceful life with all men! Find a person you can trust and tell your story to that person! Spread the love of Christ among one another! God is love so we must carry that attribute of His! Love is the most important command God wants us to operate in at all times! There is power in your words, so speak those things that aren't as if they are! Your words have the power to change your current situation! Remember to choose life and not death!

Take baby steps into your healing! Receive your healing from God. He wants you to become free from bondage and walk in your new life in Him! There isn't a better life to live than a life inside of Christ! Living in Him is a life of abundance! I pray this book was able to help you become delivered from some of your struggles! I pray the Lord continues to touch your lives in a mighty way for His divine purpose. God is not a respecter of persons...so remember God can use who He chooses for His purposes! The first will be last and the last will be first! Don't allow anyone to make you think God can't use you, or your past is too bad for God to use you! He is able, so just trust Him every step of the way! Blessings to every reader!

I would also like to encourage all parents to take the time to hear your children. It's one thing to listen to your children, but another to hear your children. So many times as parents, we believe we have all the answers. Be transparent with your children. It is okay if you don't have all of the answers. We may be the parents, but we can learn from our children the same way they learn from us. So please be diligent in hearing your children's feelings or concerns. Allow them to express their feelings to you, freely!

Everyone in my household understands the importance of encouraging one another. In my household we have standards that each person must obey too! My children had their lessons through life experiences, too. They were in the struggle with their dad and myself and witnessed the power of God in our lives. Through it all nothing was ever hidden from our children. My husband and I talked with our children about everything, and allowed them to know their voices do matter. They are able to express themselves

Chapter 16 - In Closing

in our household. My children will not think their opinions don't matter and be walked all over like a carpet. They are taught to speak up and speak out their feelings. They do this, respectfully. Every household should set a standard with high expectations for their family!

The problem with most children today is that they don't have the means to express and speak out their feelings. Everything they feel is balled up inside. They act out in various ways... usually disrespectfully. This is the reason why our children are becoming a part of the system. They aren't taught to have high expectations, or how to communicate, properly. Everything starts with the head which is the parents. Once the parents become delivered from their selfish ways, and stop taking their frustration out on the children, a change will take place. In all things there are lessons to be learned. Too many people are not learning and that's why our homes are destroyed, and the prisons are filled with our men, children, and women. Their mindset was never altered, so they still feel inadequate. It's our time as a unit to take a stand and fight for the people who don't have a voice! Remember, relationships are ruined because of miscommunication. So we should always communicate our feelings to one another. A feeling is just an emotion like I mentioned before; It does not make it a fact. So talk to one another respectfully.

The conversation can get intense, but if you don't speak out these feelings inside of you will cause much pain. You will act upon those feelings, so be wise and not quick to believe your feelings are facts. Every good relationship is built off of good communication. As I close this out be mindful of your thoughts, which produces your feelings and behavior! I know, if God did a mighty work in me and still is working on me to this day, He can do the same in you!

I have faith in you and believe God can do all things in and through you, if you only believe! Trust God, readers, and be of courage! The battle is already won and you are a survivor, so live a victorious life from this day forward!

Blessings to each reader and again I pray this book was a blessing to you!

Scripture References

Scriptures on Deliverance:

II Corinthians 10:3-5

"For though we walk in the flesh, we are not waging war according to the flesh. For the weapons of our warfare are not of the flesh but have divine power to destroy arguments and every lofty opinion raised against the knowledge of God, and take every thought captive to obey Christ."
(Bible ESV)

I Corinthians 10:13

"No temptation has overtaken you that is not common to man. God is faithful, and will not let you be tempted beyond your ability, but with the temptation he will also provide a way of escape, that you may be able to endure it."

Psalms 34:4

"I sought the Lord, and he heard me, and delivered me from all my fears."
(Bible KJV)

Ephesians 6:12

"For we don't wrestle against flesh and blood, but against the rulers, against the authorities, against the cosmic powers over this present darkness, against the spiritual forces of evil in the heavenly places." (Bible ESV)

Scriptures on Fear:

II Timothy 1:7
"For God hath not given us the spirit of fear, but of power, and of love, and of a sound mind." (Bible KJV)

Isaiah 41:10
"Fear thou not, for I am with thee: be not dismayed; for I am thy God: I will strengthen thee; yea, I will help thee; yea I will uphold thee with the right hand of my righteousness." (Bible KJV)

Scriptures on Identity:

Genesis 1:27
"So God created man in his own image, in the image of God created he him; male and female created he them." (Bible KJV)

Jeremiah 29:11
"For I know the thoughts that I think toward you. Saith the Lord, thoughts of peace, and not of evil, to give you an expected end." (Bible KJV)

Jeremiah 1:5
"Before I formed thee in the belly I knew thee, and before thou camest forth out of the womb I sanctified thee, and ordained thee a prophet unto the nations." (Bible KJV)

Scripture References

Scriptures on Being a Submissive Wife:

Proverbs 31:10-31

"*An excellent wife who can find? She is far more precious than jewels. The heart of her husband trusts in her, and he will have no lack of gain. She does him good, and not harm, all the days of her life. She seeks wool and flax, and works with willing hands. She is like the ships of the merchant, she brings her food from afar.*" (Bible ESV)

I Peter 3:1

"*Likewise, wives, be subject to your own husbands, so that even if some do not obey the word, they may be won without a word by the conduct of their wives.*" (Bible ESV)

Proverbs 18:22

"*He who finds a wife finds a good thing and obtains favor from the Lord.*" (Bible ESV)

Ephesians 5:33

"*However, let each one of you love his wife as himself, and let the wife see that she respects her husband.*" (Bible ESV)

Proverbs 12:4

"*An excellent wife is the crown of her husband, but she who brings shame is like rottenness to his bones.*"

Scriptures on Freedom:

Galatians 5:1
"For freedom Christ has set us free; stand firm therefore, and do not submit again to a yoke of slavery." (Bible ESV)

I Peter 2:16
"Live as people who are free, not using your freedom as a cover-up for evil, but living as servants of God." (Bible ESV)

Galatians 5:13
"For you were called to freedom, brothers. Only do not use your freedom as an opportunity for the flesh, but through love serve one another." (Bible ESV)

II Corinthians 3:17
"Now the Lord is the spirit, and where the spirit of the Lord is, there is freedom." (Bible ESV)

Romans 6:18
"And, having been set free from sin, have become slaves of righteousness." (Bible ESV)

Scriptures on Truth:

John 14:6
"Jesus saith unto him, I am the way, the truth, and the life: no man cometh unto the Father, but by me." Bible (KJV)

Scripture References

John 8:32
"And ye shall know the truth, and the truth shall make you free." (Bible KJV)

Ephesians 6:14
"Stand therefore having your lions girt about with truth, and having on the breastplate of righteousness." (Bible KJV)

II Timothy 2:15
"Study to shew thyself approved unto God, a workman that needeth not to be ashamed, rightly dividing the word of truth." (Bible KJV)

Scriptures on Obedience:

John 14:15
"If ye love me, keep my commandments." (Bible KJV)

Luke 6:46
"And why call ye me, Lord, Lord, and do not the things which I say?" (Bible KJV)

James 1:22
"But be ye doers of the word, and not hearers only, deceiving your own selves." (Bible KJV)

Isaiah 1:9
"If ye be willing and obedient ye shall eat the good of the land." (Bible KJV)

Scriptures on Marriage:

Matthew 19:6

"Wherefore they are no more twain, but one flesh. What therefore God hath joined together, let no man put asunder." (Bible KJV)

Ephesians 5:33

"Nevertheless let every one of you in particular so love his wife even as himself: and the wife that see reverence her husband." (Bible KJV)

Genesis 2:18-24

"And the Lord God said it is not good that the man should be alone: I will make him a help meet for him." (Bible KJV)

Scriptures on Children:

Psalms 127:3

"Lo, children are a heritage of the Lord: and the fruit of the womb is his reward." (Bible KJV)

Proverbs 22:6

"Train up a child in the way he should go: and when he is old, he will not depart from it." (Bible KJV)

Proverbs 20:11

"Even a child is known by his doings, whether his work be pure, and whether it be right." (Bible KJV)

Scripture References

Proverbs 17:6

"Children's children are the crown of old men, and the glory of the children are their fathers." (Bible KJV)

Proverbs 29:6

"The rod and reproof give wisdom: but a child left to himself bringeth his mother shame." (Bible KJV)

Scriptures on Healing:

Luke 17:9

"And he said unto him, Arise, go thy way: thy faith hath made you whole." (Bible KJV)

III John 1:2

"Beloved, I wish above all things that thou mayest prosper and be in health, even as thy soul prospereth." (Bible KJV)

I Peter 2:24

"Who his own self bare our sins in his own body on the tree, that we, being dead to sins, should live unto righteousness: by whose stripes ye were healed." (Bible KJV)

II Corinthians 7:1

"Having therefore these promises, dearly beloved, let us cleanse ourselves from all filthiness of the flesh and the spirit, perfecting holiness in the fear of God." (Bible KJV)

Scriptures on Forgiveness:

Ephesians 4:32
"And be ye kind one to another, tenderhearted, forgiving one another, even as God for Christ's sake hath forgiven you." (Bible KJV)

I John 1:9
"If we confess our sins, he is faithful and just to forgive us our sins, and to cleanse us from all unrighteousness." (Bible KJV)

Matthew 6:15
"But if ye forgive not men their trespasses, neither will your father forgive your trespasses." (Bible KJV)

Luke 6:37
"Judge not, and ye shall not be judged: condemn not, and ye shall not be condemned. Forgive, and ye shall be forgiven." (Bible KJV)

Colossians 3:13
"Forbearing one another, and forgiving one another, if any man have a quarrel against any: even as Christ forgave you, so also do ye." (Bible KJV)

About the Author

Natalie Degraffinreaidt...wife to Warren, mother of four (Airannah, Quincy, Warren lll. and Terrell), author, play writer, dancer, devoted to community service and warrior for the lost. Natalie Degraffinreaidt gave her life to Christ and is a woman after Gods own heart. Her life long journey is warring for souls. Natalie believes that through praying and fasting, she is led by the Spirit of Christ to tell her story in love and truth in bringing the people to Christ.

Natalie is building her non-profit organization (Blossoming Seeds) which is solely for people who have been mentally, verbally, sexually, emotionally, physical and drug abused. She has created programs to meet the need of the people who have suffer from such trauma.

Natalie's mission through Blossoming Seeds is ...

To bring love, knowledge, wisdom and understanding to our children and adults for this present day. We are going forth to restore what has been broken; giving our children and adults a sense of hope, believing in, learning and understanding the word of God. We will be reaching out to people of all age groups and walks of life. Our goal is to reach the need in the communities for our people. Blossoming Seeds will be creating programs to meet the need of the people. This foundation will work hard to instill the word of God in our communities, so that our people can gain hope and blossom like a rose in the concrete. This foundation is focus on helping people to become free from bondage by taking baby steps into their healing.

Scripture
1 Corinthians 3:6 *"I planted the seed, Apollo watered the plant…but it was God who made the plant to grow."*

Through telling her life story she is hoping to help others to be free from the chains of sin. She hopes to encourage every family to continue to fight for each other. There is strength in numbers. The Bible say's *"For where two or three are gathered together in my name, there am I in the midst of them."* Matthew 18:20.

Hopefully by reading this book it will free you from your guilt, shame and release you from all the hurt and pain that have kept you from being free. For whom the son sets free is free indeed.

You can find out more about Natalie at www.blossomingseeds.org.

www.ingramcontent.com/pod-product-compliance
Lightning Source LLC
Chambersburg PA
CBHW070631300426
44113CB00010B/1740